How To Play

Rock Drums

Dave Zubraski

Wise Publications

London / New York / Paris / Sydney / Copenhagen / Berlin / Madrid / Tokyo

Exclusive Distributors:
Music Sales Limited
8/9 Frith Street,
London W1D 3JB, England.

Music Sales Pty Limited
120 Rothschild Avenue,
Rosebery, NSW 2018,
Australia.

Music Sales Corporation
257 Park Avenue South,
New York, NY10010,
United States of America

Order No. AM957253
ISBN 0-7119-7338-5

(Previously published as Dave Zubraski's Rock & Heavy Metal Drums Books One & Two)

Music arranged by Andy Spiller.
Music processed by Seton Music Graphics.
Cover design by Chloë Alexander.
Photographs courtesy of LFI, Redferns and Julian Hawkins.

Printed in the United Kingdom by
Printwise (Haverhill) Limited, Haverhill, Suffolk.

How To Play

Rock Drums

Dave Zubraski

PART 1

FOREWORD

How To Play Rock Drums Parts 1 and 2 were written to take the beginner through from setting up a kit to playing in a rock band.

In Part 1 we covered basic technique, reading, a variety of fills using straight eights, triplets, shuffles, sixteenth and quarter notes.

In Part 2 we progress to the more complex and musically rewarding rhythms and fills incorporating syncopation, sixteenth notes, dotted notes, open hi-hat, tied notes, drum rudiments and different time signatures.

Some audio examples (those marked with * on the track list) are played twice on the CD, once with drums and once without. Use the first play-through to listen and learn. The second play-through, recorded without drums, is your opportunity to put what you've learned into practice by playing along with the band. Have fun!

Please note that there are two CDs accompanying this book – one for each part. When referring to the Audio Track numbers in the text, ensure you select the correct disc.

DRUM MAP

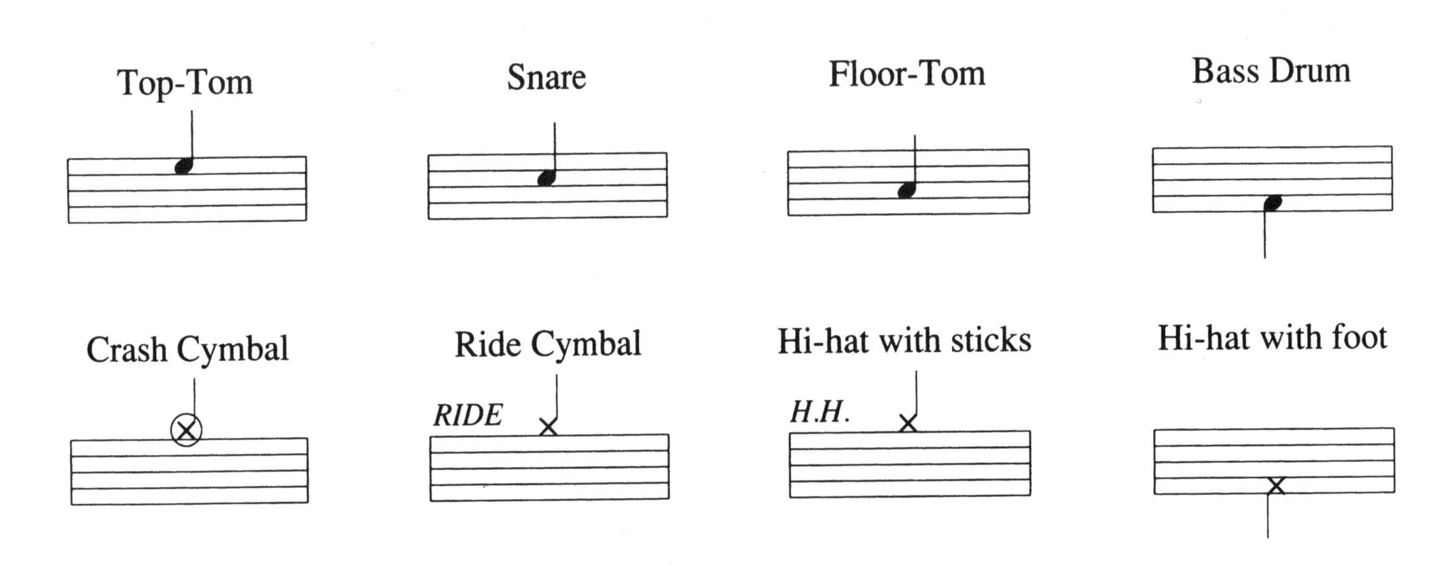

Chapter 1

SETTING UP YOUR KIT

A basic kit comprises a Bass Drum, Snare, Top-Tom, Floor Tom, Hi-Hat Stand, Snare Drum Stand, Bass Drum Pedal, 2 Cymbal Stands, 1 Pair of Hi-Hat Cymbals, 1 Ride and 1 Crash Cymbal as shown below.

When SETTING UP YOUR KIT make sure everything is within easy reach. The height of your drum stool is important as this can affect the way you play. Go for a position where your legs are relaxed and in control of the pedals.

TUNING and the choice of drum heads can make a big difference to the overall sound of a drum. The tighter you tune a drum the higher its pitch will become. This also affects the speed of the stick response. The tighter the head the faster the response.

When TUNING the SNARE drum have both heads quite tight with the snares just taut enough to stop them from rattling. If the snares are too tight it can stop them vibrating freely causing them to sound choked. Choose a head that is not too heavy as this can dull the sensitivity of the snares. I would suggest you try a Remo CS (centre spot) head for the batter (top side) and a Remo Ambassador snare for the snare head (bottom side). Most snare drums have eight or ten tension lugs, if possible buy one that has ten, as the more tension rods a drum has (this applies to all drums) the finer you will be able to tune it.

TOM-TOMS are not usually tuned to any specific notes but the smaller sizes are tuned to a higher pitch, getting lower as the sizes get larger. One thing to keep in mind when tuning the toms is to make sure they all have the same decay time.* You can do this by playing one beat on each tom and listening to how long the note rings. Using a Zero Ring or a small piece of tissue paper (as damping) taped to the top head, positioned away from the area you are playing on, you can adjust the decay time. More damping will result in a shorter decay, less damping will result in a longer decay.

The BASS drum is generally tuned as low as possible without losing its tone. To achieve this tighten the heads only enough to take the wrinkles out. A pillow or blanket placed inside the drum against the back head is often used as damping to cut the ring down and produce a good solid thud.

There are two basic ways of playing the bass pedal. One way is to have the whole foot flat on the pedal (as shown in photograph 1), the other way is to raise the heel of your foot and only use your toes (as shown in photograph 2).

Sometimes a combination of both methods is used. You might find using the toe method is easier for playing faster patterns, I suggest you try both ways to see which is the more comfortable for you.

1.

2.

* The decay time determines how long the note will sound before it dies away.

When adjusting the tension spring on the bass pedal don't have it too tight or too loose. There should be just enough tension in the spring so that when you rest your foot on the pedal, the weight of your foot is enough to move the beater onto the head.

Bass drum beaters are usually made from felt or wood. A hard felt beater is the most commonly used as this produces a fast response and a good tone.

CARE and MAINTENANCE

A few points on general CARE and MAINTENANCE. A well maintained kit will last longer, look better and, what is more important, be less likely to let you down on a gig or recording session.

1. Keep all tension rods, screws, springs, snare release etc., lightly oiled.

2. As the SNARES are the most delicate part of the kit, try not to touch them unnecessarily and do not lay anything on top of them as this can cause the thin strands of wire to bend. If this happens they will vibrate unevenly causing an annoying buzz.

3. CYMBALS can be cleaned (not too often) with cymbal cleaner (obtained at most music stores) or washed with warm soapy water using a sponge, making sure you completely dry the cymbal after washing. Be careful not to use anything abrasive e.g. metal cleaner, scouring pad etc. as this can damage a cymbal. Do not clamp your cymbals to the stands too tightly as this can prevent them from vibrating freely and possibly cause them to crack.

4. Most DRUM HEADS are made of plastic and are very durable. However, with constant use they will gradually lose their tone and become less responsive and should be replaced. To change a drum head, first unscrew (using a drum key) and remove all the tension rods, then lift off the counter hoop. Remove the old head and fit the new one, replace the counter hoop and tension rods, then tune the head (as described on pages 5 and 6) by tightening each tension rod in sequence (as shown in the diagram below) by one turn, until the required sound and feel are obtained.

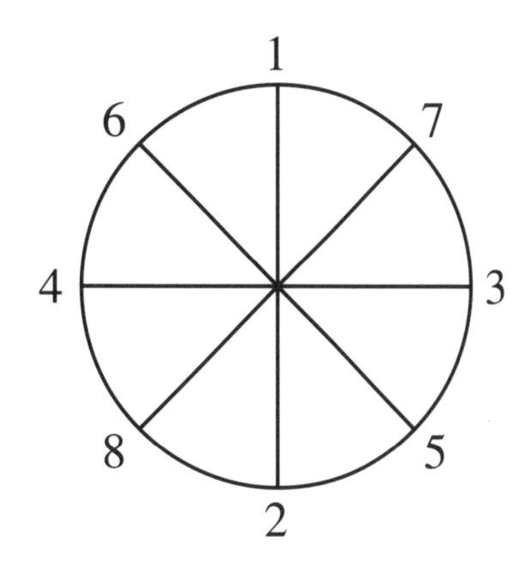

5. Do not STORE your drums too near to a heat source e.g. radiator, open fire etc.

6. When transporting your kit a set of waterproof FIBRE CASES is recommended. These come in all different sizes so make sure you know the measurements of your drums before buying them.

HOLDING the STICKS

There are two basic ways of holding the sticks. One way is the Matched Grip, where both sticks are held in the same way. The other is the Traditional Grip. Most rock drummers favour the Matched Grip (for power and speed) as shown below.

Matched Grip

Right Hand

With the palm of your right hand facing towards the floor, hold the stick about one third of the distance from the butt end, so it pivots between the ball of the thumb and the joint of the first finger, (as shown in photograph A).

A

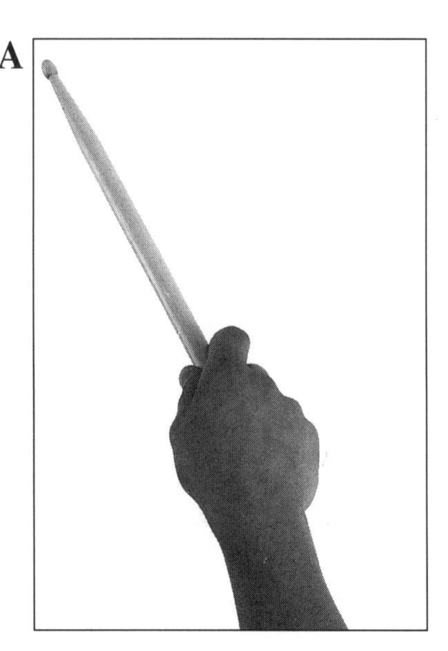

B

Let your first finger curl around the stick, then bring your second, third and fourth fingers gently around onto the stick to guide and stabilise it.
(See photographs B and C).

C

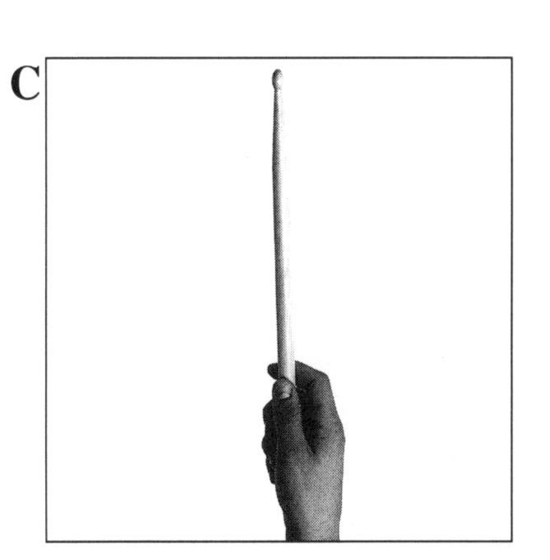

Left Hand

The left hand grip should be exactly the same as the right hand. Try to keep both hands and fingers as relaxed as possible.

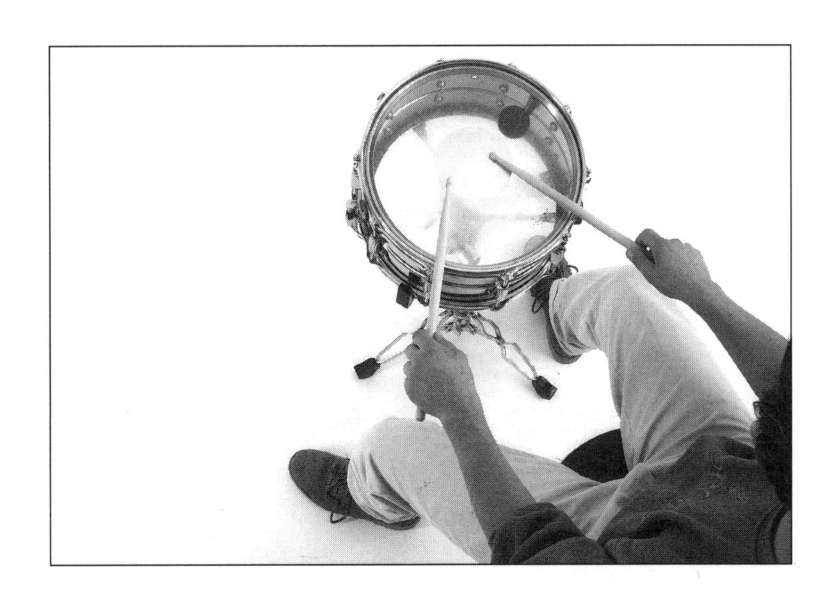

READING MUSIC

Music is written on five parallel lines called a STAVE. It is divided into BARS by bar lines. Below is one bar of music. This is also called a MEASURE.

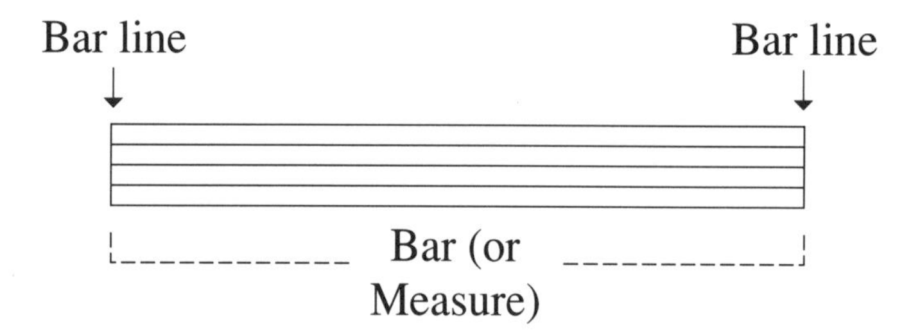

A double bar line || indicates the beginning and end of a section, e.g. Chorus, Verse, Instrumental etc.

A repeat sign 𝄆 𝄇 means you play all the bars that fall between two such signs twice.

At the beginning of a piece of music is a sign called a CLEF. There are several clefs, but in Rock and Pop music only two clefs are used, the Treble and Bass. Drum music is written in the Bass clef. Percussion with a definite pitch such as the Marimba, Crotales, Kalimba etc., are written in the Treble clef.

Within each measure are combinations of notes or their equivalent rests. (A rest is a silent note which you count but do not play.) Below are the names of the notes we shall be using.

WHOLE NOTE *also called a* SEMIBREVE

HALF NOTE *also called a* MINIM

QUARTER NOTE *also called a* CROTCHET

EIGHTH NOTE *also called a* QUAVER

SIXTEENTH NOTE *also called a* SEMIQUAVER

When two or more eighth notes follow in succession they are tied together by a thick line called a beam.

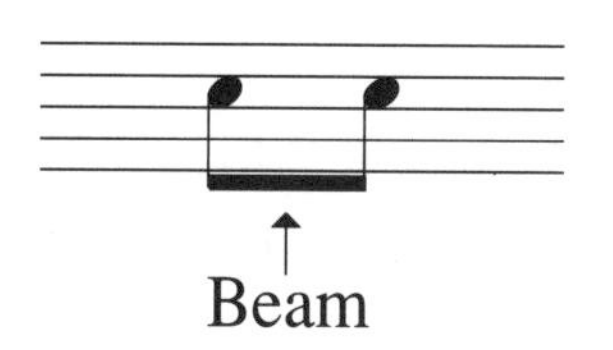

Two or more sixteenth notes are tied together by two beams.

Below is a table showing the RELATIVE VALUES of these notes.

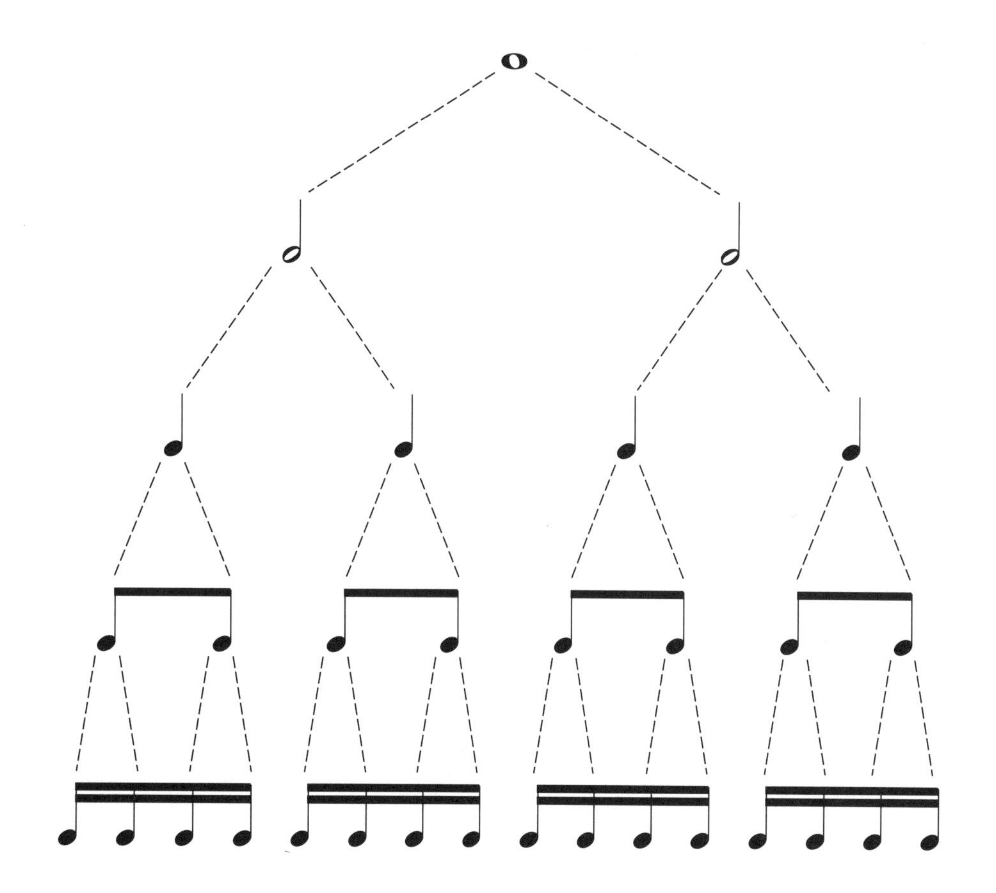

RESTS

For every note in music e.g. Quarter note, Eighth note, Sixteenth note etc., there is an equivalent rest. Below is a table showing all the rests we shall be using.

Note the Whole note rest HANGS from the bar line whereas the Half note rest SITS on the line.

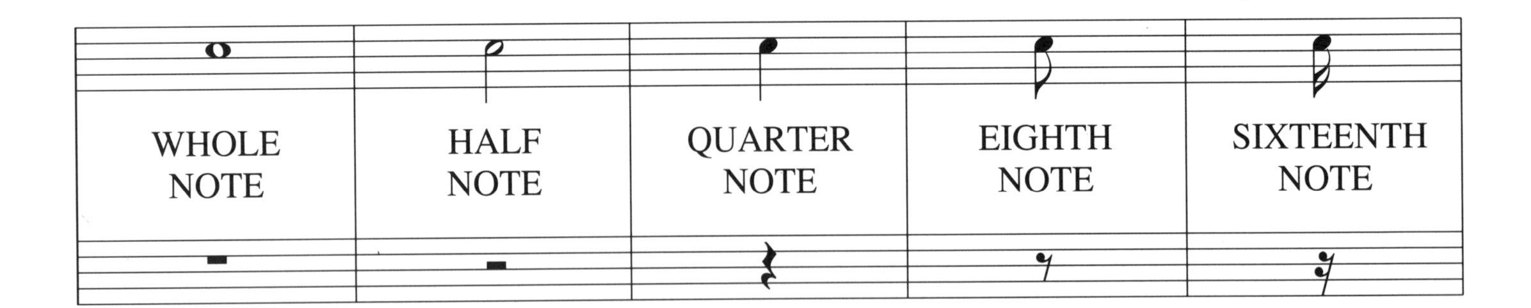

Each note has a COUNT all of its own. Below are the counts given to some of the notes we will be using.

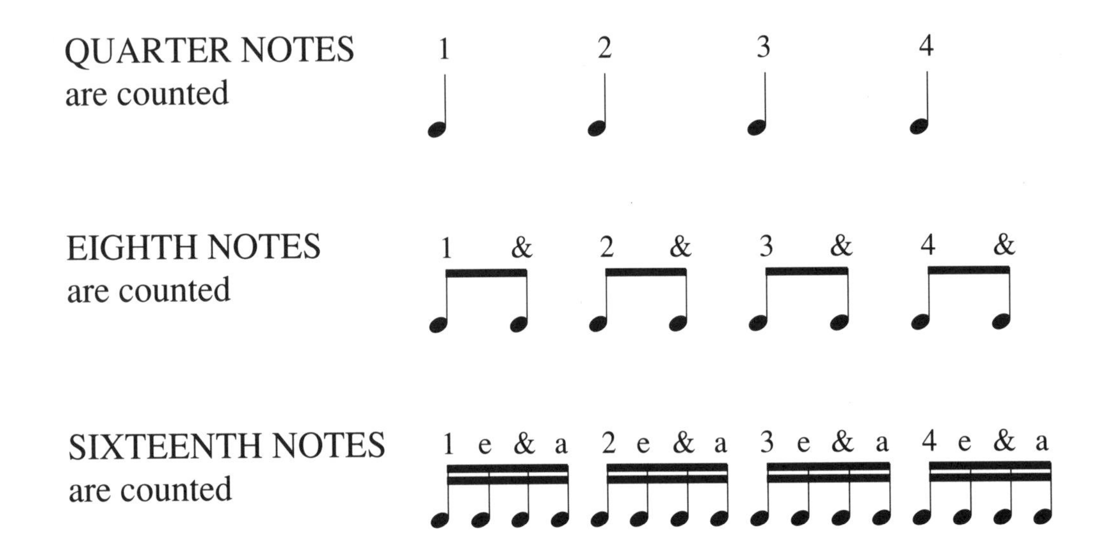

At the beginning of each piece of music there is a TIME SIGNATURE, for example $\frac{4}{4}$.

The top number 4 tells us how many beats there will be in a bar.

The bottom number 4 tells us what sort of beats they are.

Therefore, a time signature of $\frac{4}{4}$ has four quarter notes or their equivalent in a bar.

Each drum is written on a different line within the stave, as shown below.

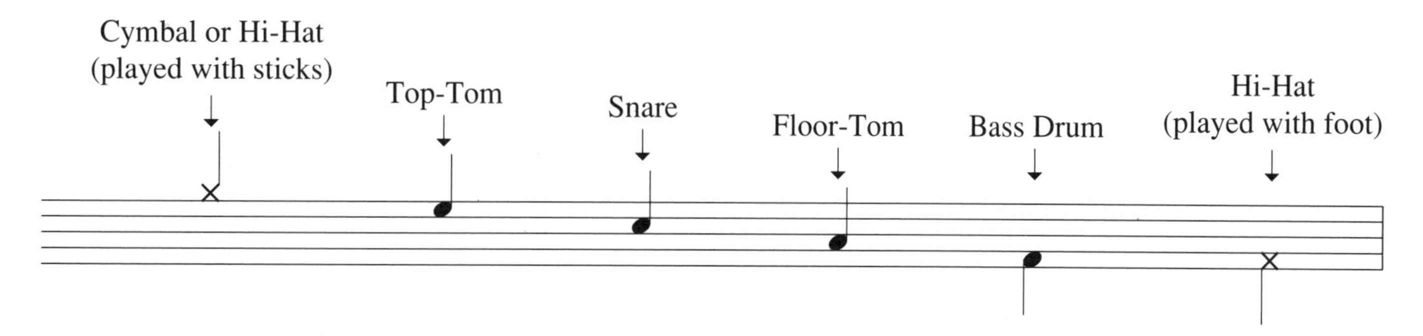

When the word 'Ride' is written on the cymbal line, this means the cymbal pattern is to be played on the ride cymbal as shown here.

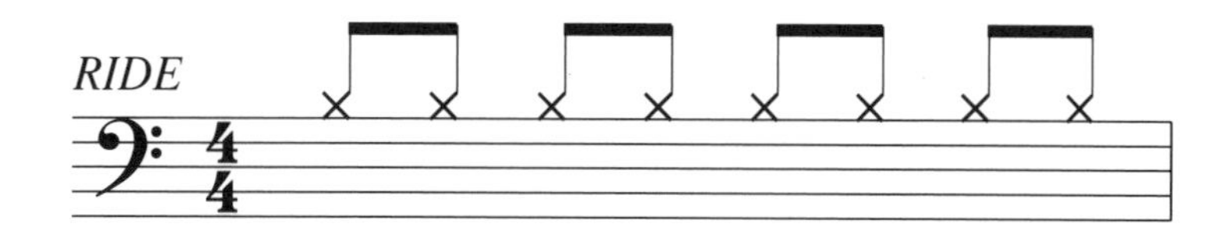

Similarly, when 'H.H.' is written, the cymbal pattern is to be played on the closed hi-hat (usually with your right hand) as shown in this example.

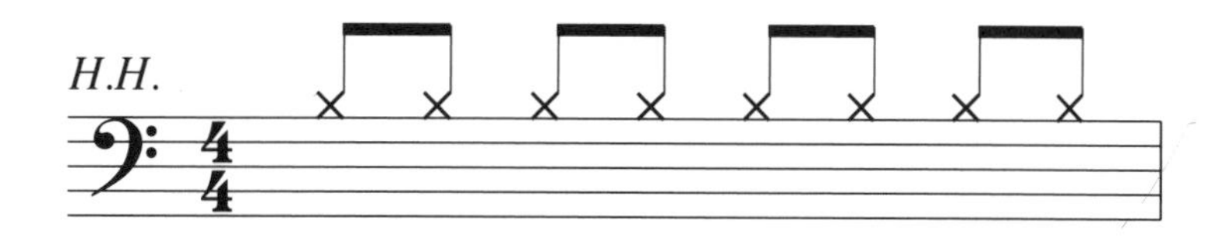

If a crash cymbal is to be played it is shown with a circle around the note ⊗.

In the next example the cymbal rhythm is to be played on the closed hi-hat with only the first beat to be played on the crash.

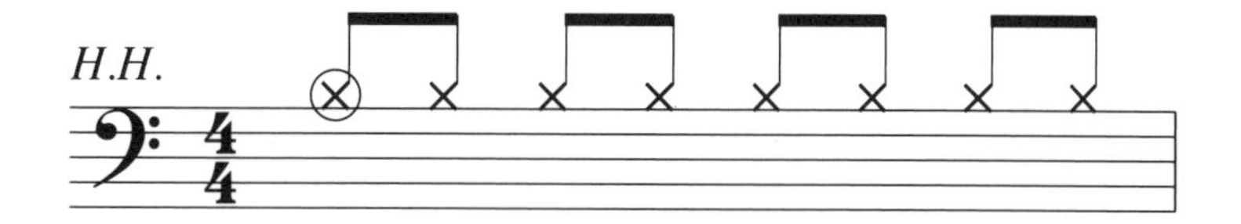

Chapter 2

PRACTICE

The main role of the drummer is to keep time. This means being able to play a piece of music from start to finish without speeding up or slowing down. It is useful to practise all the exercises in this book with and without the use of a metronome.

BPM is an abbreviation for beats per minute. This is used to indicate the tempo at which a piece of music is to be played, e.g. 120 bpm would indicate a tempo of 120 quarter note beats per minute (or the equivalent). When playing along with a metronome remember that each swing of the pendulum from left to right and vice versa is equal to one quarter note (or the equivalent).

Always start each exercise at a slow tempo, speed does not matter at the beginning. What does matter is EVENNESS of playing. Count slowly and evenly through the exercise first, then play and count simultaneously. Once you are satisfied with your performance you can then practise the exercise at a new increased tempo. Always stop and take a short rest before trying a new tempo, never increase or decrease gradually (unless specified) as this will lead to bad habits later on. If you feel yourself becoming tense at any time, stop and take a short rest before continuing to practise. All the exercises in this book have been written assuming you are right-handed. However, if you are left-handed play the exercises using the reverse hands and feet.

Concentrate your practice on one exercise at a time. Don't be in too much of a hurry to move on to the next exercise, stay with the one you're working on until you are confident you can play it reasonably well.

You may find some exercises take more practice than others, but as you progress through the book and your co-ordination gets better, each exercise will improve. Try to practise every day rather than spending a lot of time one day then none the next.

Listening to, and watching other drummers play are important parts of learning, but as with any creative form you should strive to be ORIGINAL. After you have mastered all the exercises in this book you can play them with your own variations, e.g. by changing a cymbal or bass drum part etc. you can create a rhythm of your own.

Don't be afraid to hit the drums. It is important to be able to play everything at different volumes, from Pianissimo (very soft) to Fortissimo (very loud). To get the right feel of a rock rhythm you have to play with enough power to sound confident and solid while being relaxed at the same time. This only comes with PRACTICE.

COUNTING

Exercise 1 Audio Track no. 2

Every exercise in this book is demonstrated on the accompanying Audio Track and starts with a one bar count. In Chapter 2 (exercises 2–5) all the audio examples are demonstrated at two tempos, slow and medium, so you can hear clearly how the rhythms are constructed and (with practice) how they will sound at a faster tempo. The following examples are demonstrated at one tempo (medium) only.

In exercise 1 we will concentrate on COUNTING. As this piece of music is written in 4/4 you will hear a four beat count at the start. (If it were written in 3/4 you would hear a three beat count etc.) Keep the hi-hat closed with your left foot on the pedal and play the quarter note closed hi-hat pattern with your right hand, say the count (which is written above each note) 1, 2, 3, 4, throughout the track. Make sure each count coincides with each beat played. If you get out of time with the music, stop, and start again from the beginning.

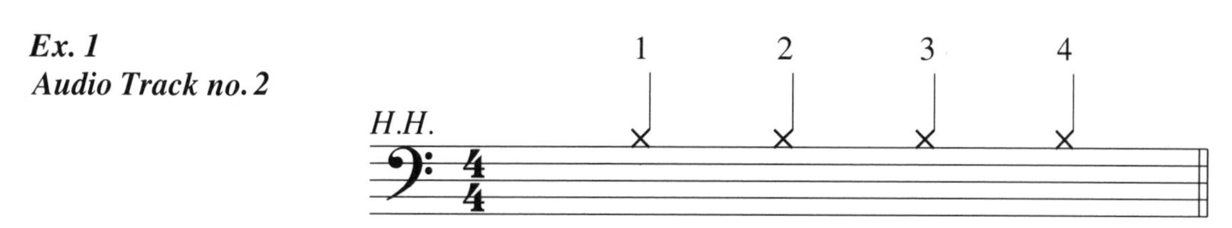

For extra practice start anywhere in audio track no. 2 and try to pick up the count as before, 1, 2, 3, 4, etc.

When you are listening to the radio or a record try counting to the music. This should not, however, be practised in a public place as it can be very annoying and could possibly cause a somewhat angry response!!

BASIC HEAVY METAL ROCK RHYTHMS

Exercise 2 Audio Track nos 3–8

Exercise 2a consists of a bar of eighth notes played on the closed hi-hat with your right hand. When playing along to a metronome remember that each beat of the metronome is equal to one quarter note, so in exercise 2a you play two eighth notes to every beat of the metronome. Don't forget to say the count as you play.

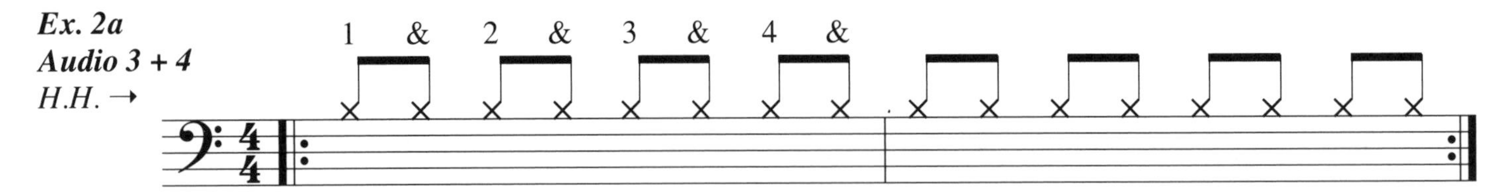

Exercise 2b Audio Track nos 5 and 6

In exercise 2b we have added the snare drum (played with your left hand) on beats 2 and 4*. Let the stick bounce back off the drum head after each beat is played. Avoid pushing the stick into the drum head as this can cause the head to dent.

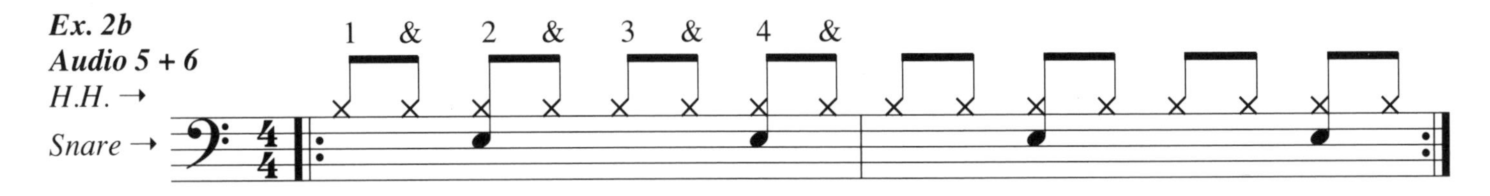

Exercise 2c Audio Track nos 7 and 8

In exercise 2c we have added the bass drum (played with your right foot) on beats 1 and 3** (Note the quarter note rests 𝄽 on beats 2 and 4). When playing the bass and snare parts, make sure every beat falls exactly in time with the hi-hat pattern.

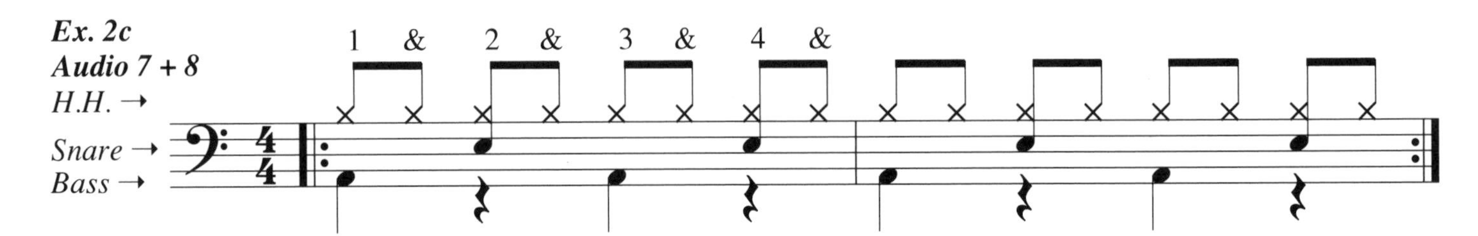

Practise these patterns at different tempos (in stages of 5 bpm) from 50 bpm to 130 bpm.

---

* Beats 2 and 4 are called the OFF BEATS or BACK BEATS.

** Beats 1 and 3 are called the ON BEATS.

Note the double bar line and repeat signs at the beginning and end of each exercise.

BASIC HEAVY METAL ROCK RHYTHMS WITH BASS DRUM VARIATIONS

Exercise 3 Audio Track nos 9–16

In exercise 3 we have four different bass drum patterns. The hi-hat and snare play the same throughout, only the bass drum changes. The hi-hat should remain constant in both volume and tempo. Note the eighth note rests 𝄾 used in exercises 3c and 3d.

Ex. 3a
Audio 9 + 10

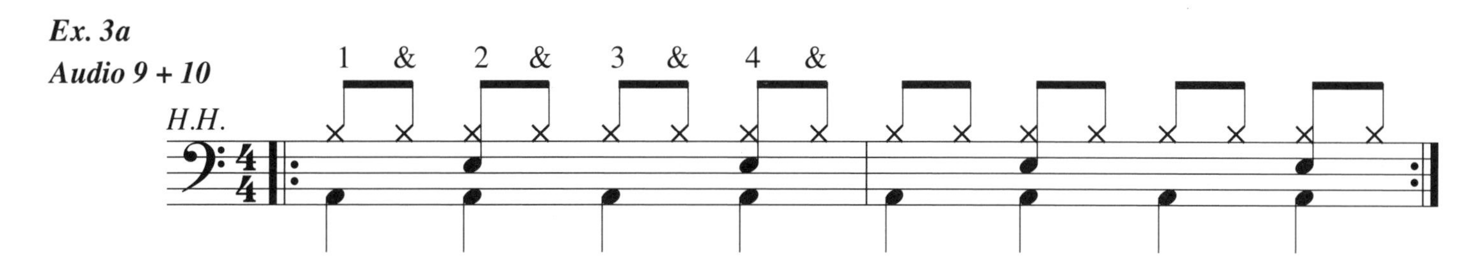

Ex. 3b
Audio 11 + 12

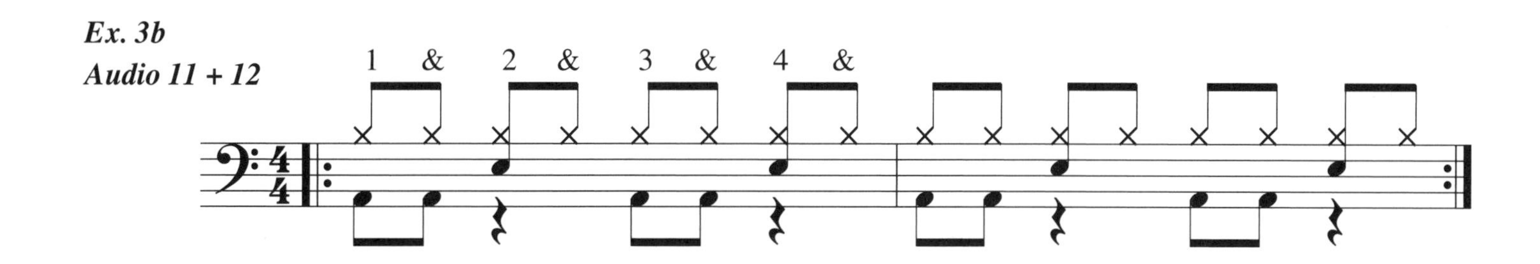

Ex. 3c
Audio 13 + 14

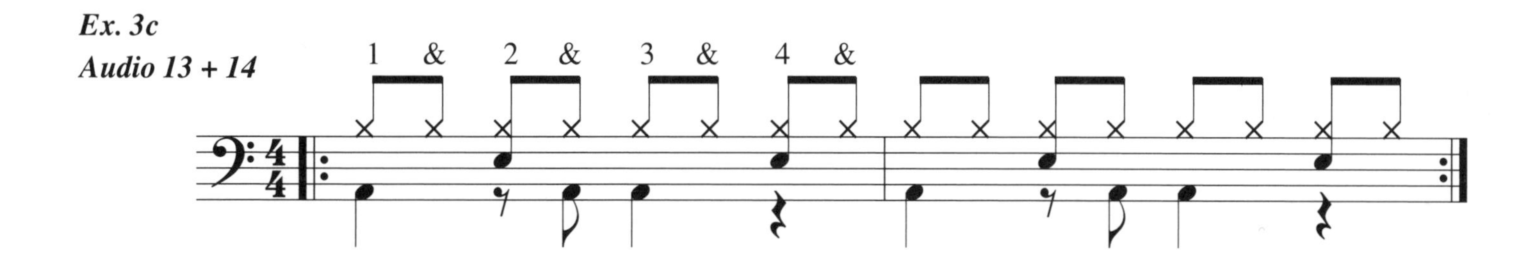

Ex. 3d
Audio 15 + 16

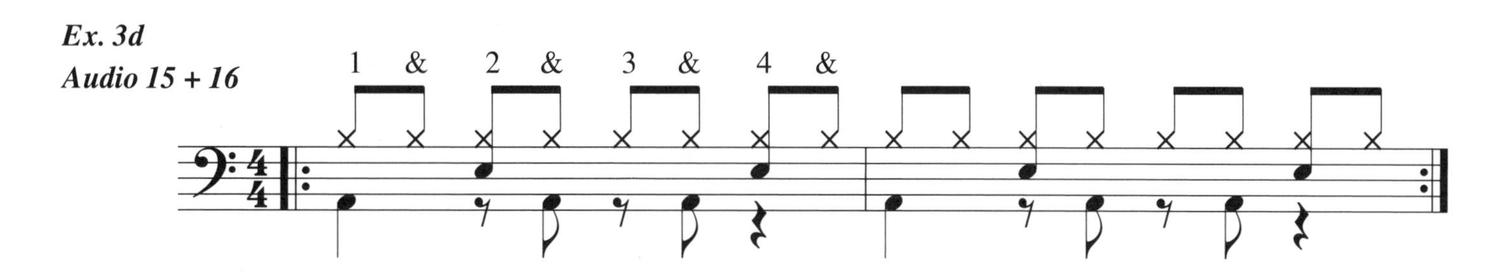

When practising these rhythms, try to play each exercise for two or three minutes without speeding up or slowing down.
For extra practice play the hi-hat pattern on the floor tom (with your right hand), this will give a much heavier feel to the rhythm.
Practise these exercises at different tempos from 50 bpm to 130 bpm.

BASIC HEAVY METAL ROCK RHYTHMS WITH SNARE DRUM VARIATIONS

Exercise 4 Audio Track nos 17–24

In exercise 4 we have four different snare drum patterns. The bass drum and hi-hat play the same throughout, only the snare drum changes.

Ex. 4a
Audio 17 + 18

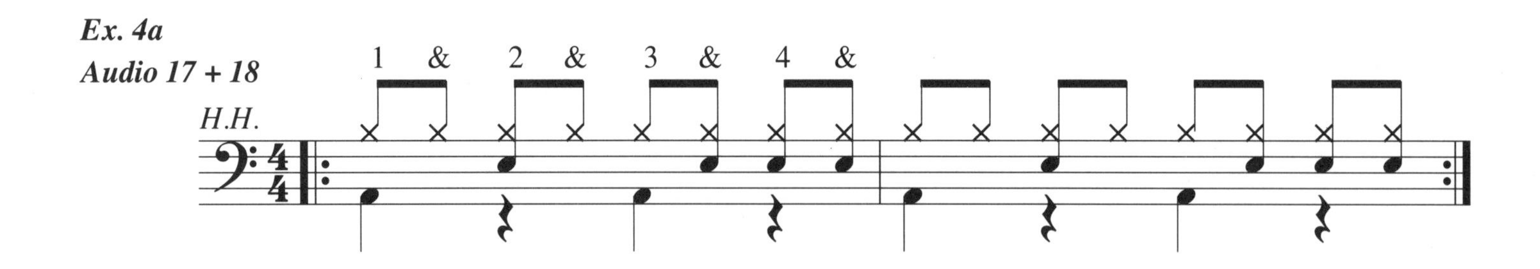

Ex. 4b
Audio 19 + 20

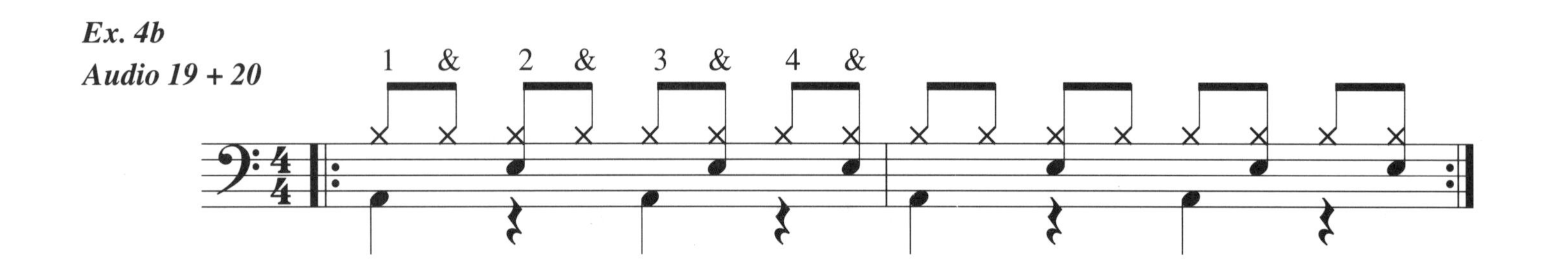

Ex. 4c
Audio 21 + 22

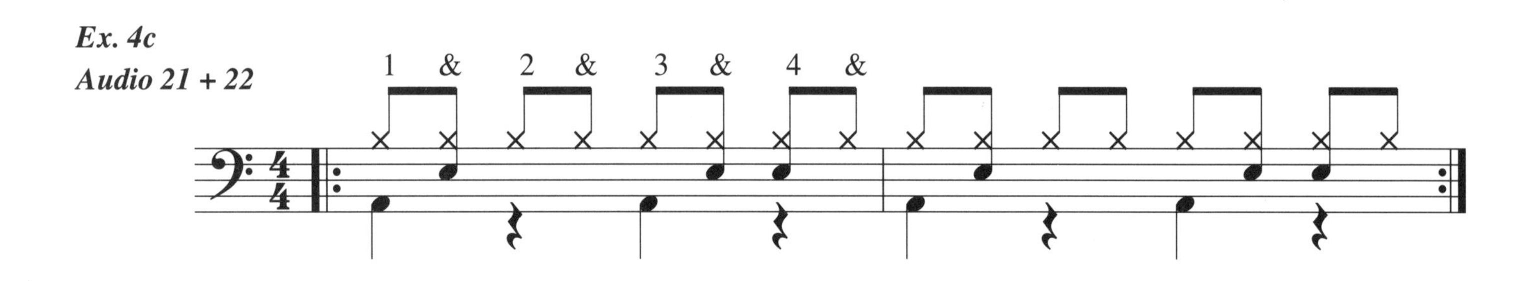

Ex. 4d
Audio 23 + 24

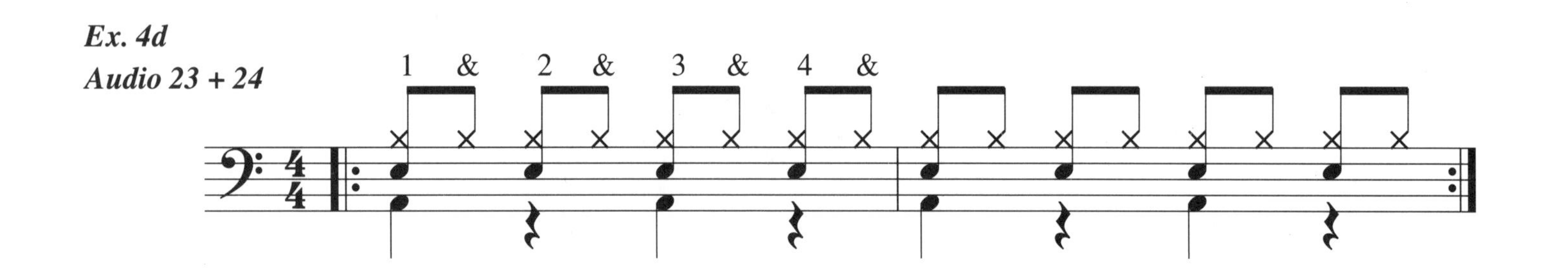

Practise these exercises at different tempos, from 50 bpm to 130 bpm.

BASIC HEAVY METAL ROCK RHYTHMS WITH SNARE AND BASS DRUM VARIATIONS

Exercise 5 Audio Track nos 25–32

In exercise 5 we have four rhythms combining different bass and snare drum patterns. Note in exercise 5d the snare drum plays only on beat 3, this gives a "half time" feel to the rhythm.

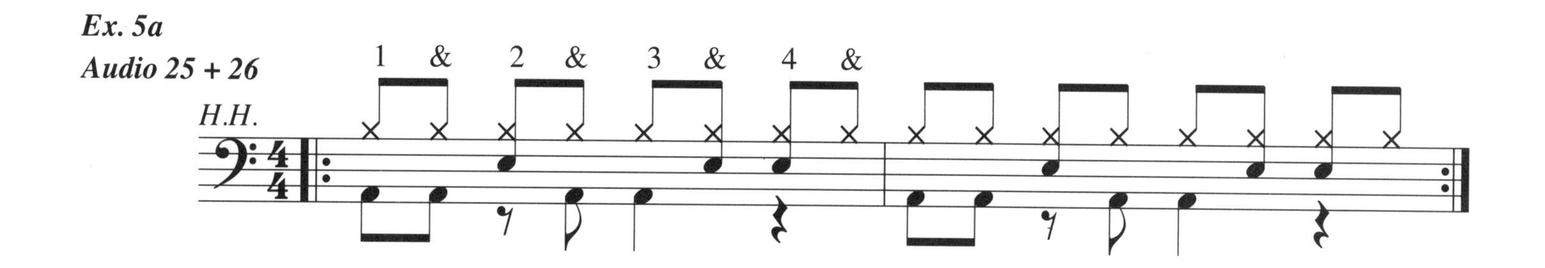

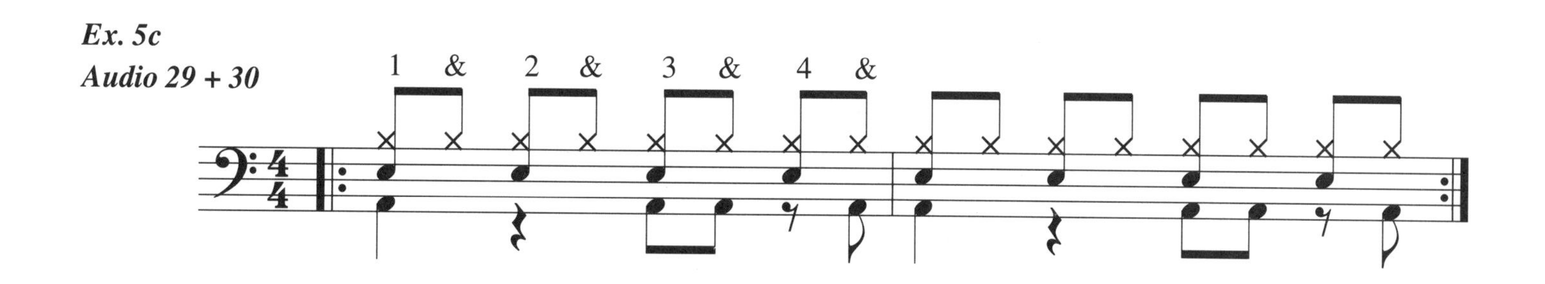

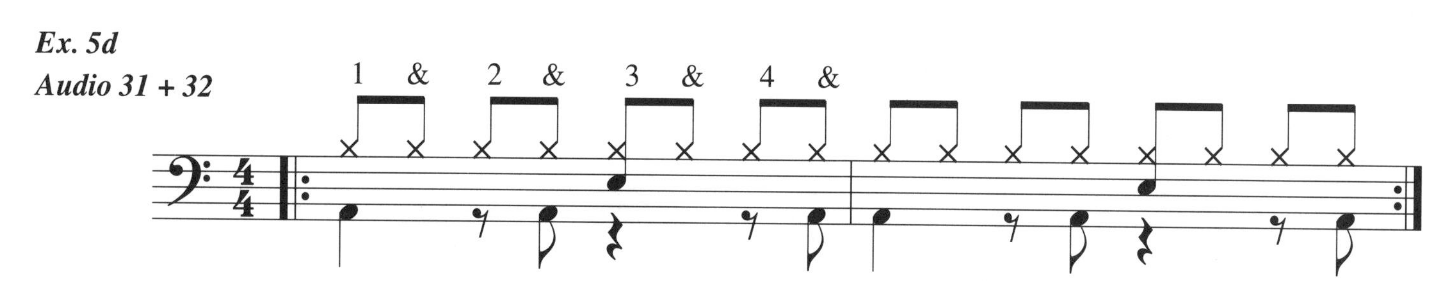

When practising these rhythms it is important to get the right balance within the kit. To obtain a good heavy rock feel, the bass and snare drum should be equal in volume with the cymbal pattern a little lower in volume as you will hear on the audio tape examples.
Practise these exercises at different tempos, from 50 bpm to 130 bpm.

JOINING RHYTHMS

Exercise 6 Audio Track nos 33 (demonstration) and 34 (minus drums)

Having practised all the previous rhythms as separate exercises it is important to be able to play smoothly from one pattern to another without losing the groove or changing the tempo. Exercise 6 is written in $\frac{4}{4}$ and consists of three eight bar sections, A, B, and C.
In place of writing every bar we have used one bar repeat signs

In PART A we play a basic rock rhythm as practised in exercise 2c.
In PART B we play another eight bars of the rhythm as practised in exercise 5b.
In PART C we move back to the first rhythm as practised in exercise 2c.

Note the numbers 4, 8, etc. written above the bars. When playing a lot of repeat bars these numbers help to show you at a glance where you are in the music.
For extra practice play through exercises 5a to 5d without stopping.

HEAVY METAL ROCK RHYTHMS
USING QUARTER NOTE HI-HAT PATTERNS

Exercise 7 Audio Track no. 35

So far we have used eighth note hi-hat patterns. In exercise 7a we have the hi-hat playing a heavy quarter note pattern falling on beats 1, 2, 3, 4. The snare plays the off beats 2 and 4 with the bass falling on beats 1 and 3 (the on beats).

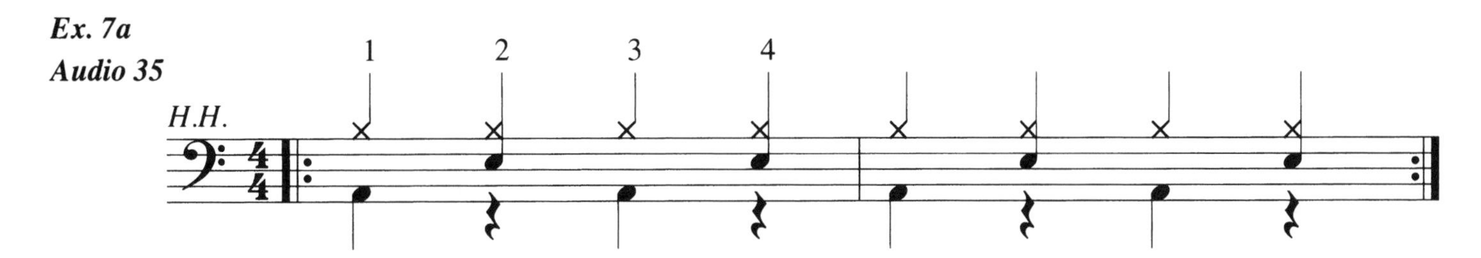

When playing along to the metronome remember that each beat of the metronome is equal to one quarter note, so in exercise 7a and 7b you will play one quarter note on the closed hi-hat to every beat of the metronome.

Exercise 7b Audio Track no. 36

In exercise 7b we have a bass drum variation using the quarter note hi-hat pattern throughout.

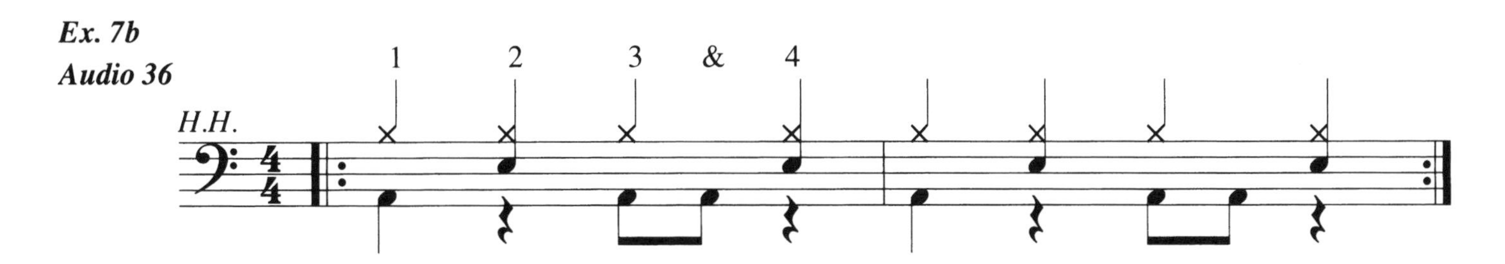

Practise these rhythms at different tempos from 70 bpm to 130 bpm.

HEAVY METAL ROCK RHYTHMS USING QUARTER NOTE HI-HAT PATTERNS (CONTINUED)

Exercise 8 Audio Track nos 37–40

In exercise 8 we have four more bass drum variations. When playing these rhythms make sure your hi-hat does not follow the bass drum pattern. Note in exercise 8d the snare only plays on beat three, this gives a "half time" feel to this rhythm.

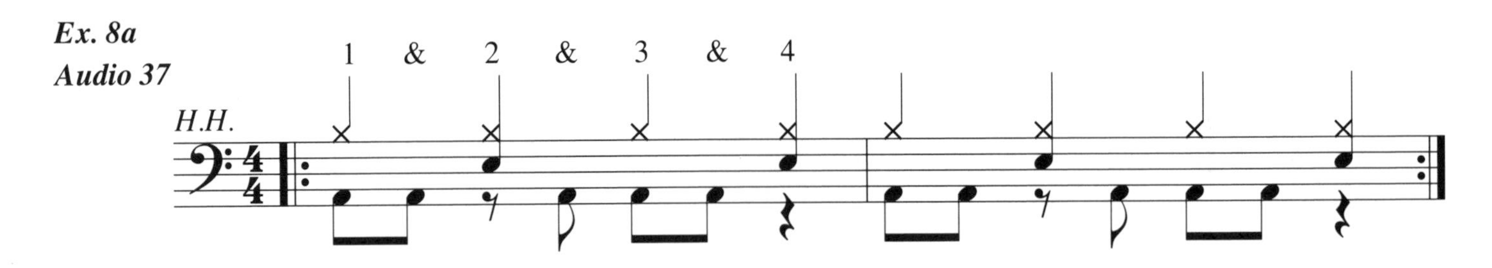

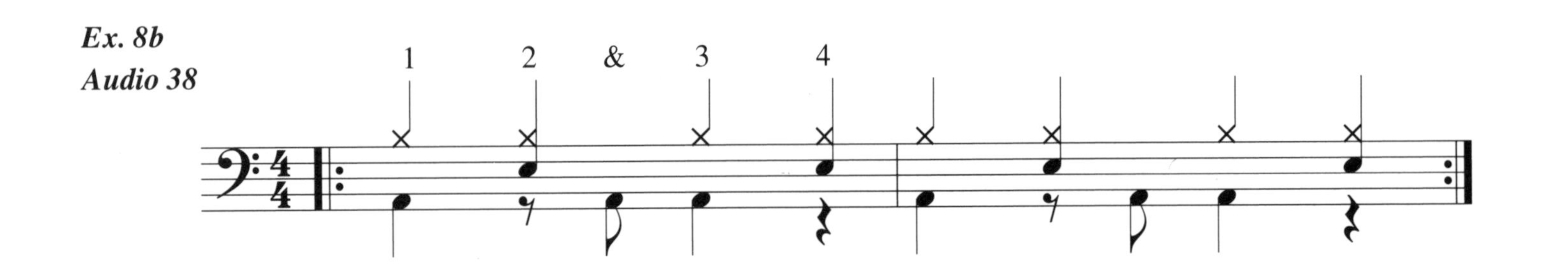

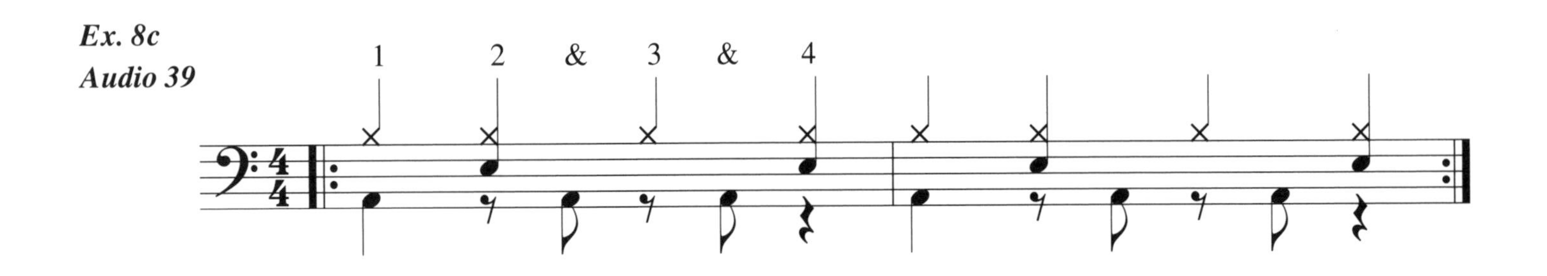

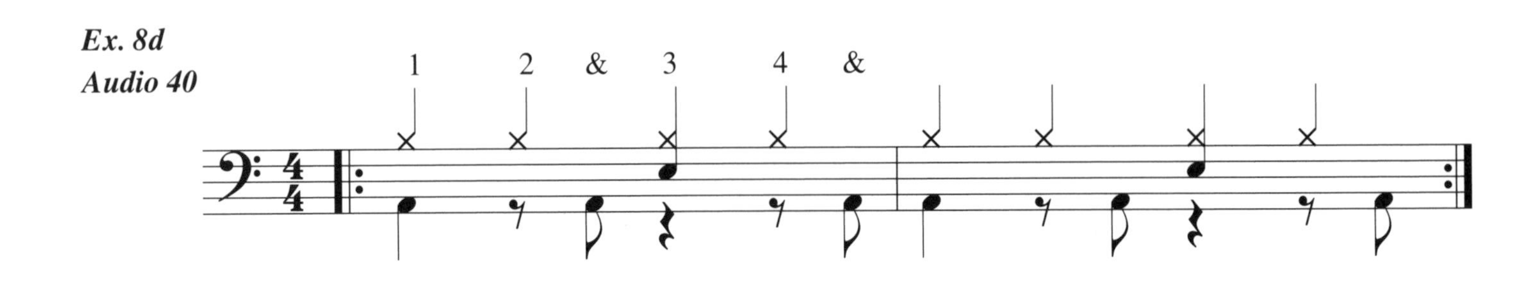

For extra practice play the hi-hat pattern on a cowbell or the bell of the ride cymbal.
Practise these exercises at different tempos, from 70 bpm to 130 bpm.

HEAVY METAL ROCK RHYTHMS
USING EIGHTH NOTE RIDE CYMBAL PATTERNS

Exercise 9a Audio Track no. 41

In exercise 9a we have an eighth note cymbal pattern played on the ride cymbal with your right hand. The hi-hat is played with your left foot and closes on beats 2 and 4 . The snare is played with your left hand and falls (simultaneously with the hi-hat) on beats 2 and 4. The bass drum plays a quarter note pattern on beats 1, 2, 3, 4.

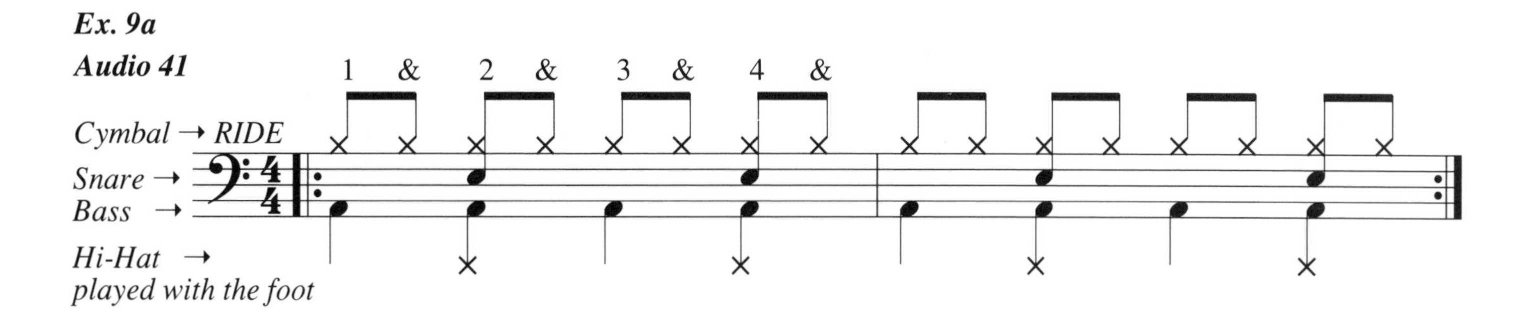

Exercise 9b Audio Track no. 42

In exercise 9b we have a bass drum variation. The hi-hat closes on beats 2 and 4 as in exercise 9a.

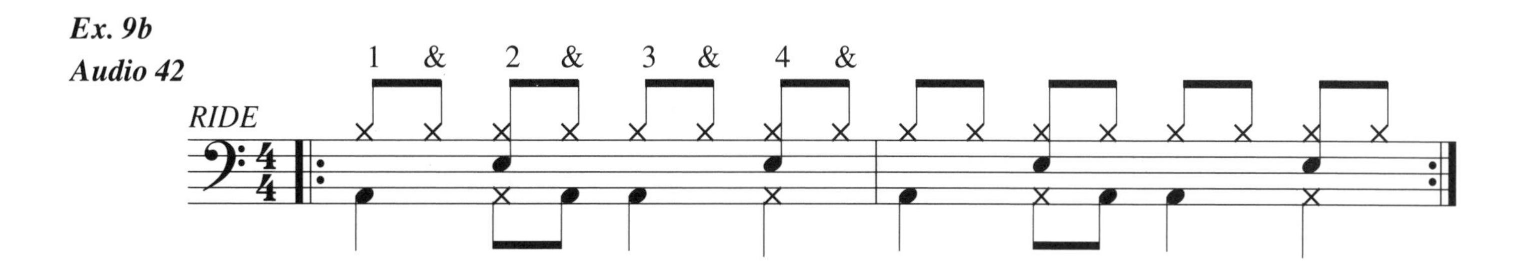

Play the ride cymbal half way between the bell and the outer edge, let the stick bounce back off the cymbal after each beat.
Practise these rhythms at different tempos from 50 bpm to 130 bpm.

HEAVY METAL ROCK RHYTHMS USING EIGHTH NOTE RIDE CYMBAL PATTERNS (CONTINUED)

Exercise 10 Audio Track nos 43–46

In exercise 10 we have four more variations. When playing rhythms 10c and 10d make sure your hi-hat does not follow the snare drum pattern but closes on beats 2 and 4 only.

Ex. 10a
Audio 43

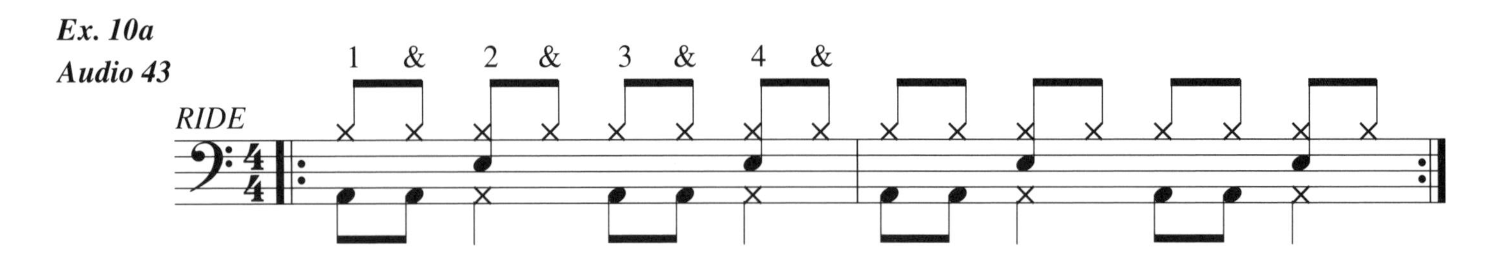

Ex. 10b
Audio 44

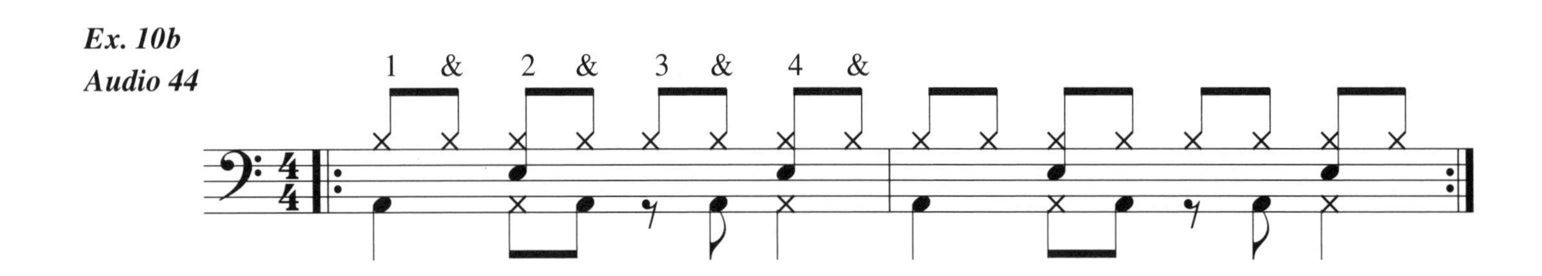

Ex. 10c
Audio 45

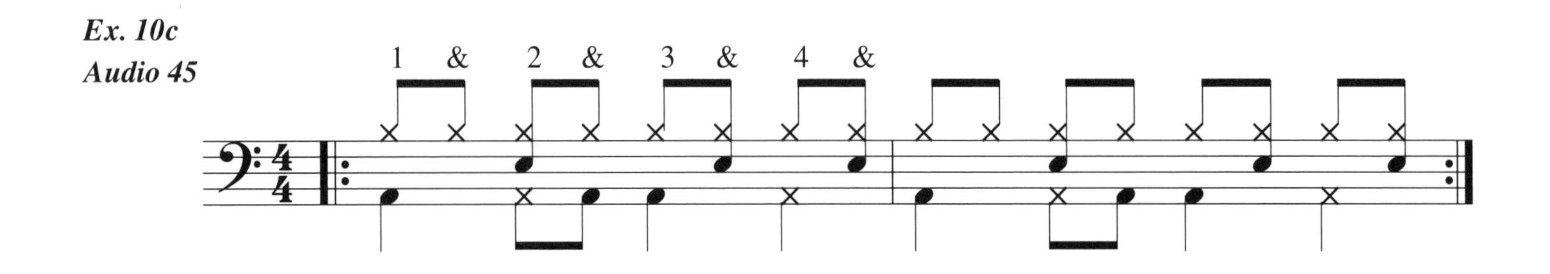

Ex. 10d
Audio 46

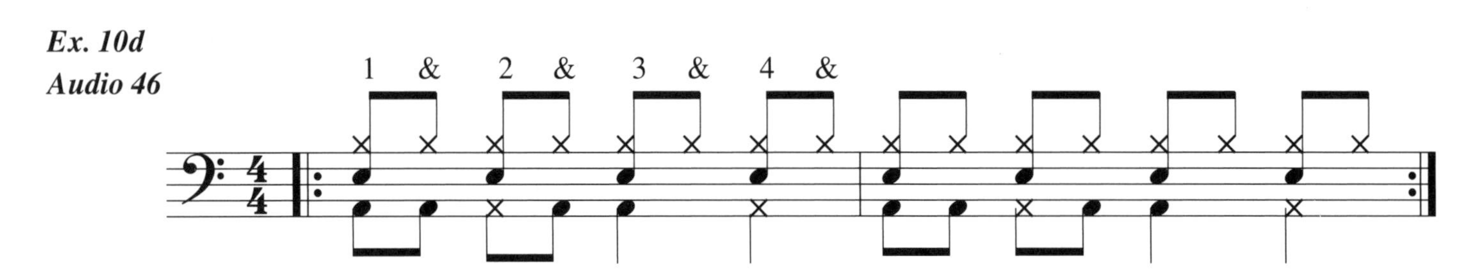

For extra practice play each bar twice (as written), then without stopping play the rhythm on the closed hi-hat instead of the ride cymbal. Make sure you do not speed up or slow down when changing between the ride and closed hi-hat.
Practise these exercises at different tempos from 50 bpm to 130 bpm.

CONSTRUCTING A SONG

Exercise 11 Audio Track nos 47 and 48

Having practised all the rhythms in chapter 2 it is important to be able to use them in the context of a song. The next track demonstrates the use of four of the rhythms we have practised.

When playing with a band it is essential to reflect the mood of the music in your drumming. This can be achieved by playing different patterns for different sections, moving a cymbal rhythm from the ride to the closed hi-hat, using dynamics (varying the volume and intensity of your playing within a piece of music). All these changes help to create the overall mood.

It is especially important to listen to the bass player as the bass and drums are the foundation of any rhythm section. Always make sure your bass drum pattern integrates well with the bass player. In exercise 11 (audio track no. 47) listen to how the bass drum pattern locks in with the bass guitar.

Exercise 11 is written in $\frac{4}{4}$. It consists of four sixteen bar sections.

In PART A we play the quarter note hi-hat pattern as practised in exercise 8c.

PART B moves to the ride cymbal pattern as practised in exercise 10a.

PART C has a half time feel as practised in exercise 5d.

PART D we move back to the ride cymbal and play the rhythm as practised in exercise 10d.

Note the repeat signs at the beginning and end of sections A, B and D.

Note the one bar drum break at bar 48. We shall be exploring Drum Fills in more depth in chapters 3 and 5.

All the rhythms we have practised in this chapter have been used on many records. For some good examples of how these basic rhythms can sound, listen to GUNS N' ROSES "Sweet Child Of Mine", ZZ TOP "Give Me All Your Loving", METALLICA "Never Never Land" and LED ZEPPELIN "In The Evening".

Exercise 11 Audio Track nos 47 and 48

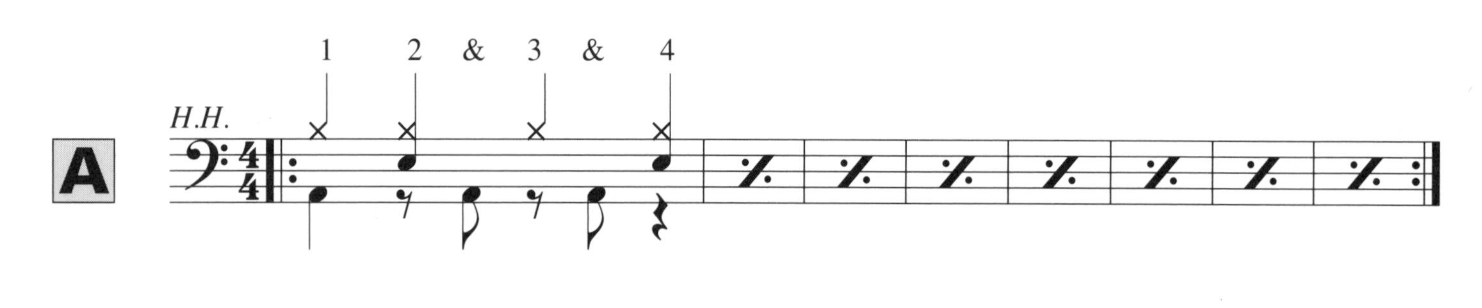

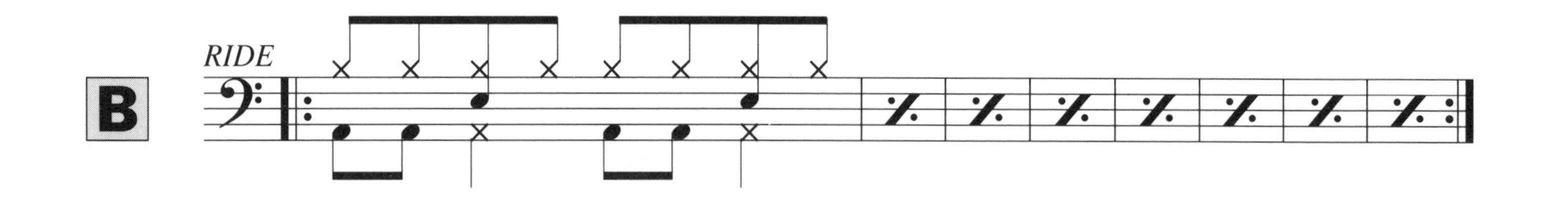

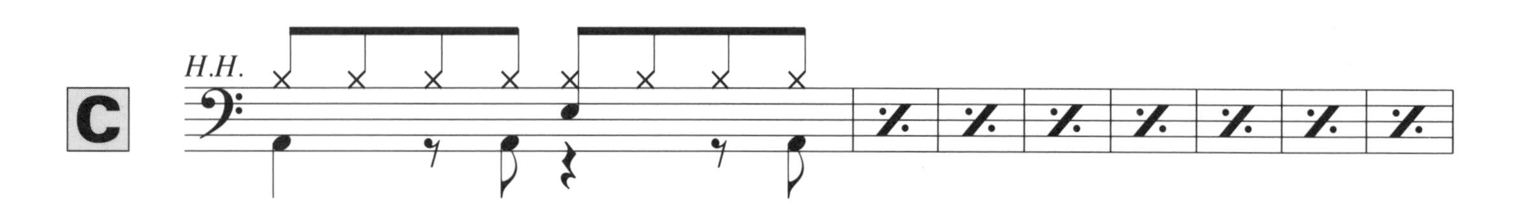

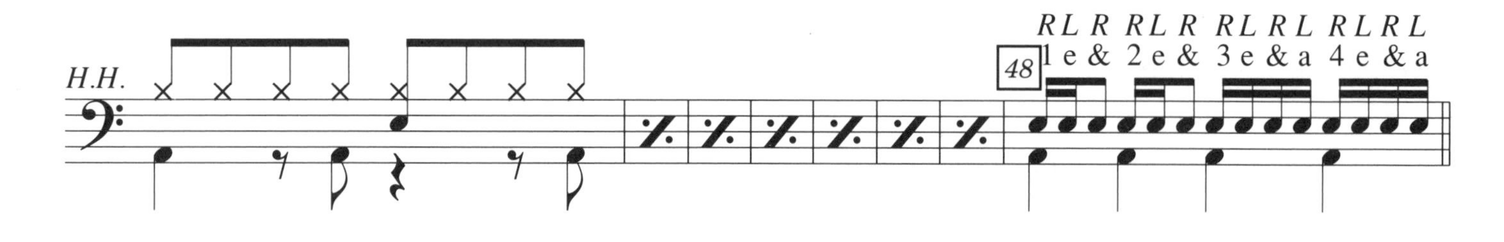

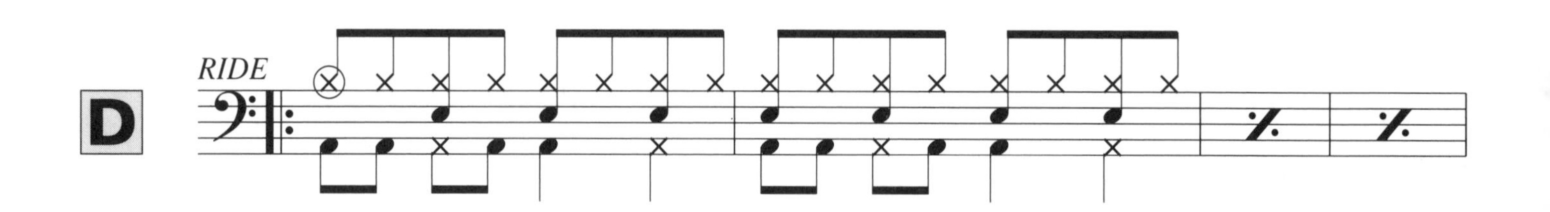

Chapter 3

BASIC SNARE DRUM FILLS

Exercise 12 Audio Track no. 49

Exercise 12 is played on the snare. Say the count (written above each note) aloud as you play. Make sure each note coincides with each beat played.

The sticking is written above each note, R = Right hand, L = Left hand.

Start with both sticks at the same height above the drum. Bring each stick down in a straight line and then let it bounce back off the drum head returning to the starting position, this will produce a clear, clean note.

Practise exercise 12 at different tempos starting at 50 bpm.
When you can play the whole exercise proficiently increase the tempo (in stages of 5 bpm) up to 120 bpm. Make sure you take a short break before each increase in tempo.When playing along to the metronome remember that each beat is equal to one quarter note. Therefore, in exercise 12a you will play one quarter note to every beat of the metronome, in exercise 12b you play two eighth notes and in exercise 12c you play four sixteenth notes.

The above exercise is written with SINGLE STROKE sticking. This means playing one beat with each hand e.g., R L R L etc.

For extra practice play this exercise using DOUBLE STROKE sticking.
This means playing two beats with each hand e.g., R R L L etc.

BASIC SNARE DRUM FILLS (CONTINUED)

Exercise 13 Audio Track no. 50

In exercise 13 we have added the bass drum and hi-hat to the snare part. First play the bass drum and hi-hat whilst saying the count, then add the snare part. You will notice the bass drum falls on beats 1, 2, 3, 4 throughout with the hi-hat falling on beats 2 and 4 throughout.

Make sure your bass drum maintains a constant tempo whilst the snare part doubles up each bar, playing 4, 8 then 16 beats.

For extra practise play exercise 13 using Double Stroke sticking (as shown).

Practise this exercise at different tempos from 50 bpm to 120 bpm.

Exercise 14 Audio Track no. 51

Exercise 14 is a two bar exercise. Exercise 14a is a bar of rhythm and exercise 14b is a one bar drum fill.

Exercise 14b is composed of a bar of sixteenth notes played on the snare. Make sure your bass drum and hi-hat maintain a constant beat throughout both bars.

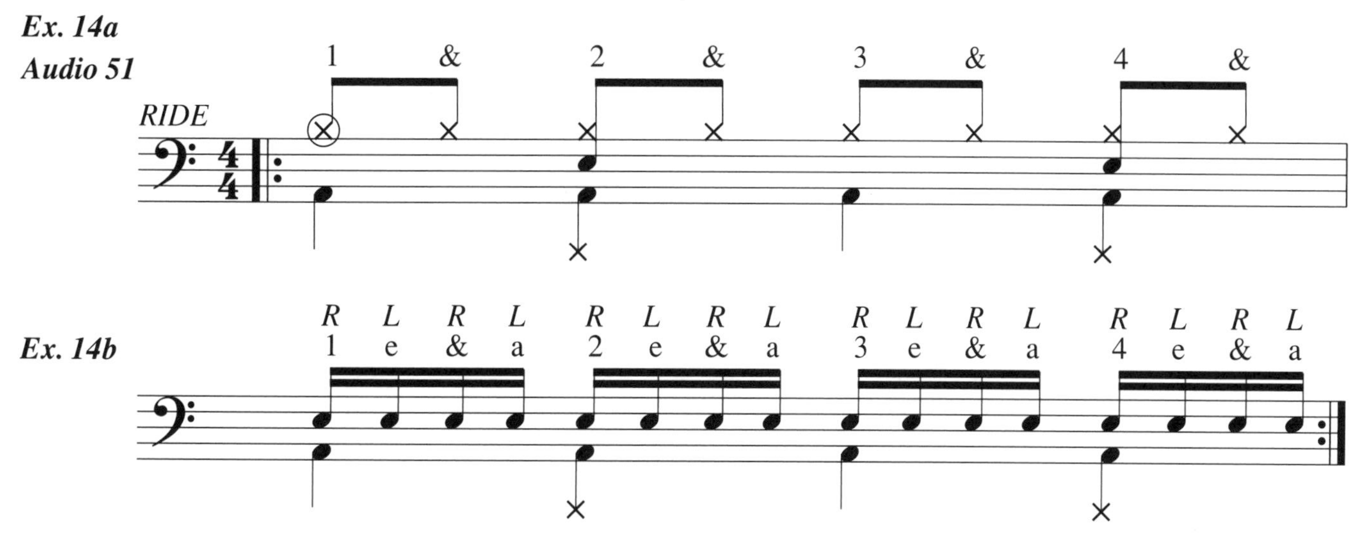

Exercise 15 Audio Track no. 52

In exercise 15b we have a variation on the one bar drum fill. The fourth sixteenth note of each group of four (which would have been played with your right hand) has been replaced by an eighth note on the &, which is equal to two sixteenth notes.

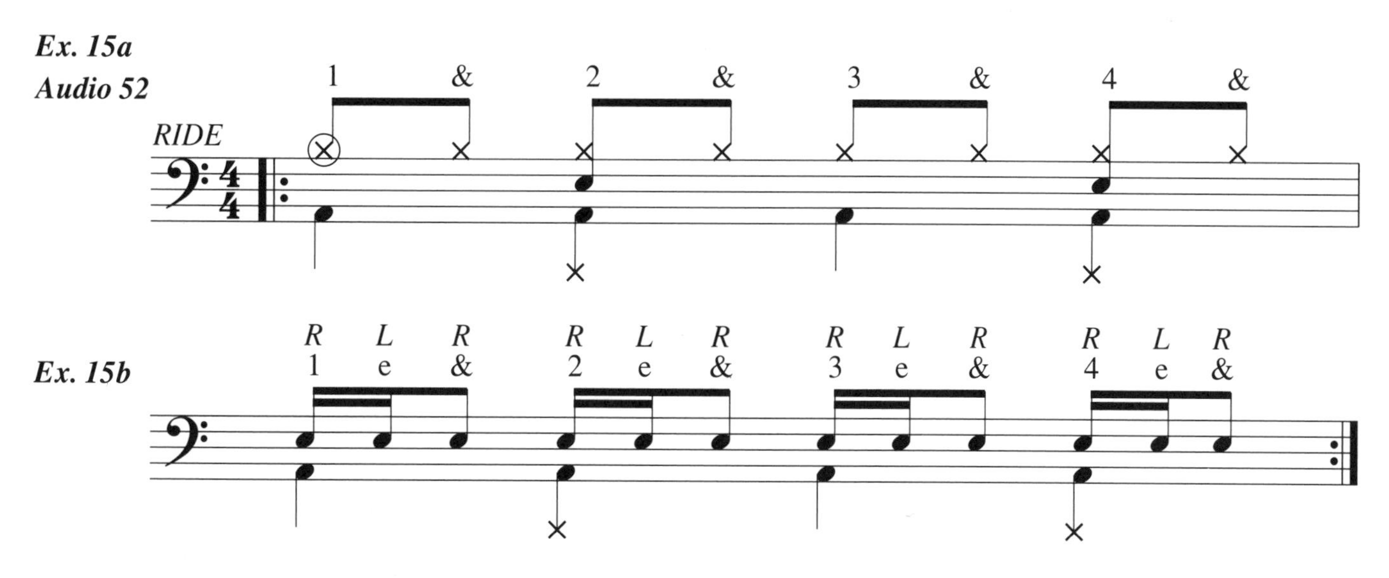

For extra practice play both exercise14b and 15b snare parts using Double Stroke sticking (R R L L etc.).
Note the crash cymbal (played with your right hand) on beat one in exercises 14a and 15a.
Practise this exercise at different tempos from 60 bpm to 130 bpm.

BASIC SNARE DRUM FILLS (CONTINUED)

Exercise 16 Audio Track no. 53

In exercise 16b the second sixteenth note of each group of four (which would have been played with your left hand) has been replaced by an eighth note on the first beat which is equal to two sixteenth notes.

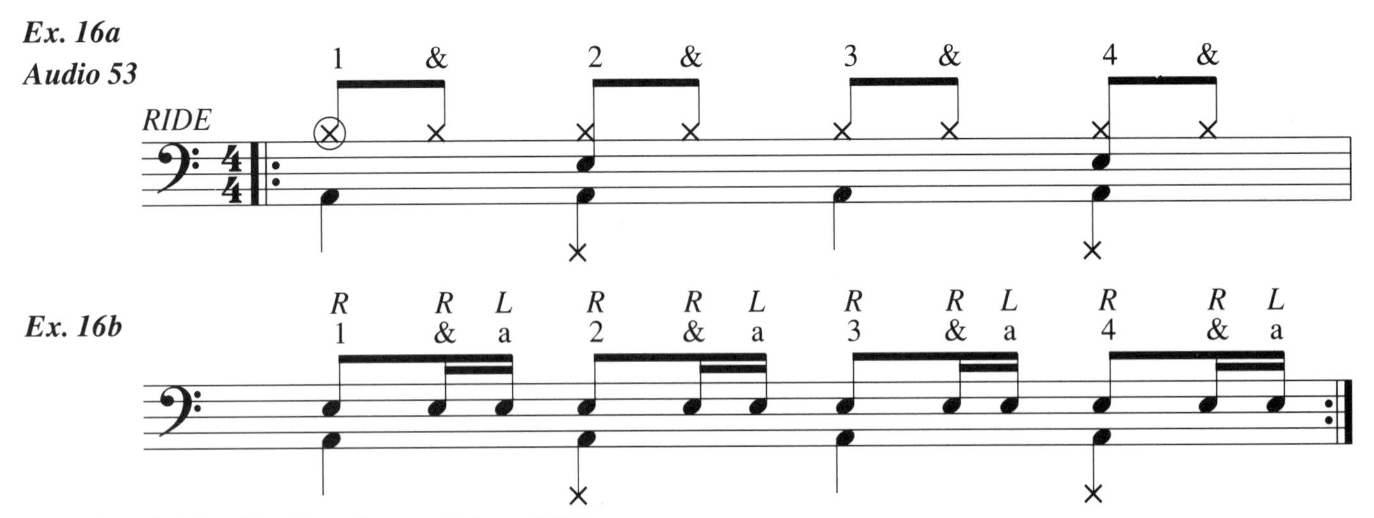

Exercise 17 Audio Track nos 54 and 55

In exercise 17 we have three bars of rhythm followed by a one bar drum fill.

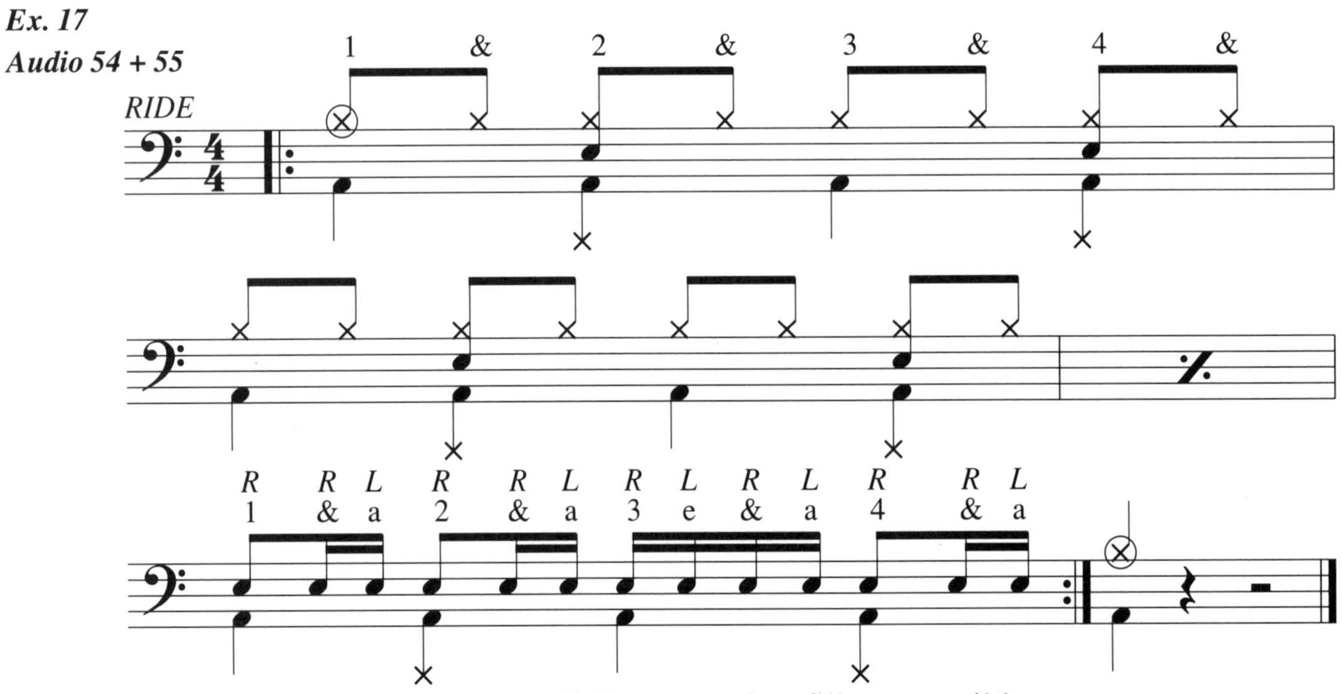

For extra practice try to create as many different one bar fills as possible.

For extra practice in exercises 14, 15 and 16, play THREE bars of rhythm before playing the one bar drum fill. This turns these exercises into four bar patterns giving you a better feel as to when a drum fill should be played.

So far all the drum fills have been played on the snare, in chapter 5 we will practise them around the kit.

Chapter 4

TRIPLETS

A triplet is a group of three equal notes usually played in the time of one beat. They have a figure 3 placed above or below each group to make them easily recognisable.

Triplets have a very different feel from any of the notes we have used so far. The count for eighth note triplets is:

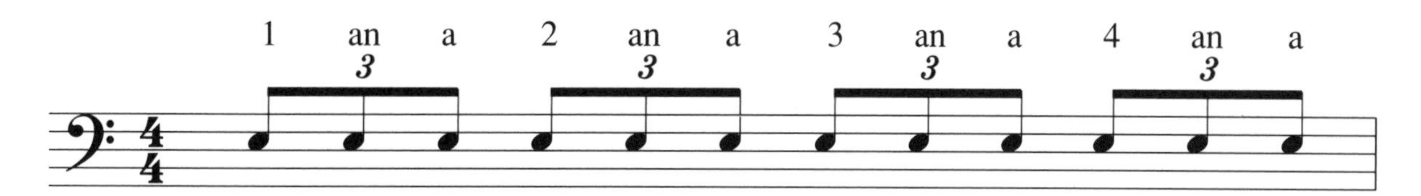

The table below shows the eighth note triplet's relative value to the other notes we have used.

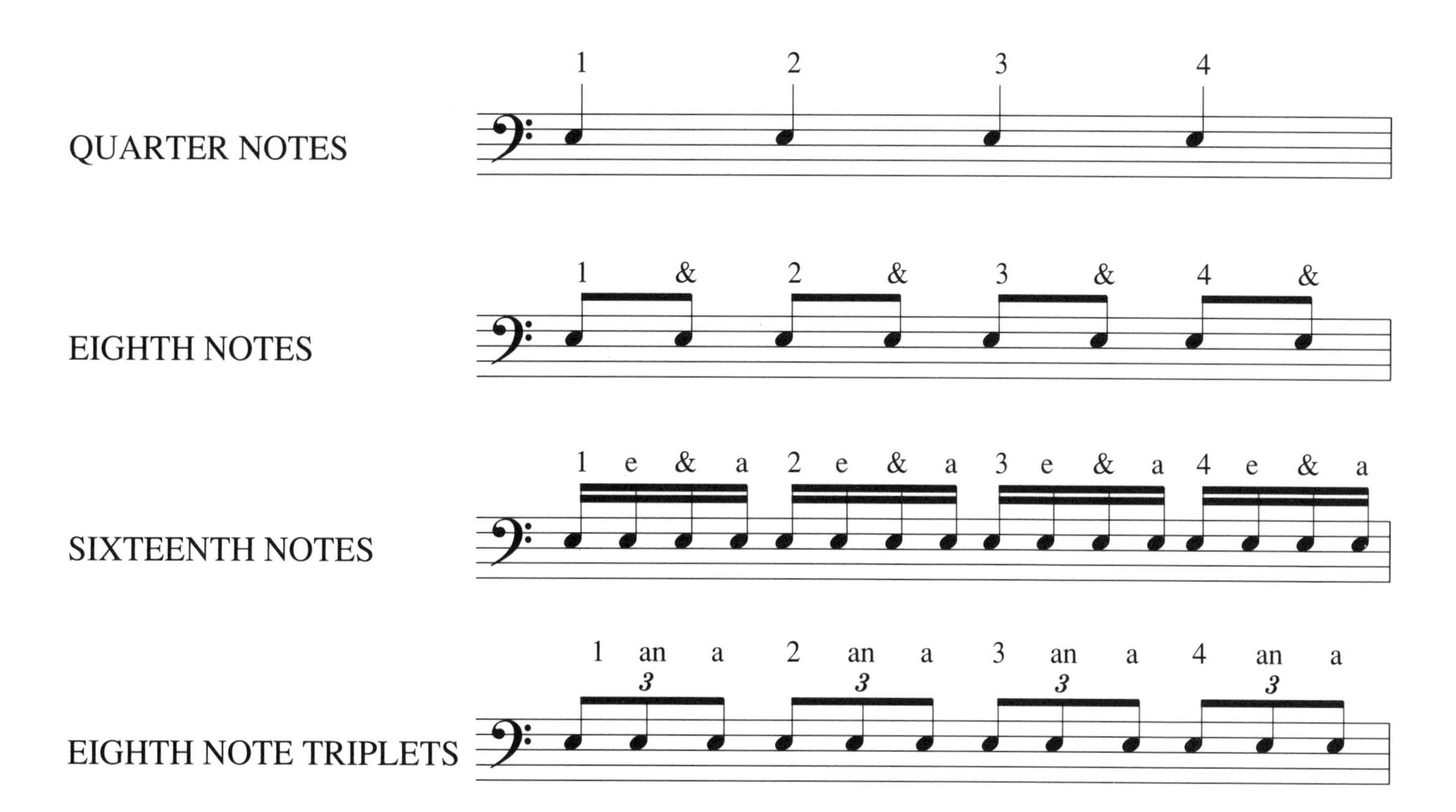

Exercise 18 Audio Track no. 56

In exercise 18 we have four bars of eighth note triplets played on the snare. Three beats with each hand R R R L L L. Say the count evenly, making sure each count coincides with each beat played. The bass drum maintains a steady four quarter notes to the bar, with the hi-hat falling on beats 2 and 4.

Ex. 18
Audio 56

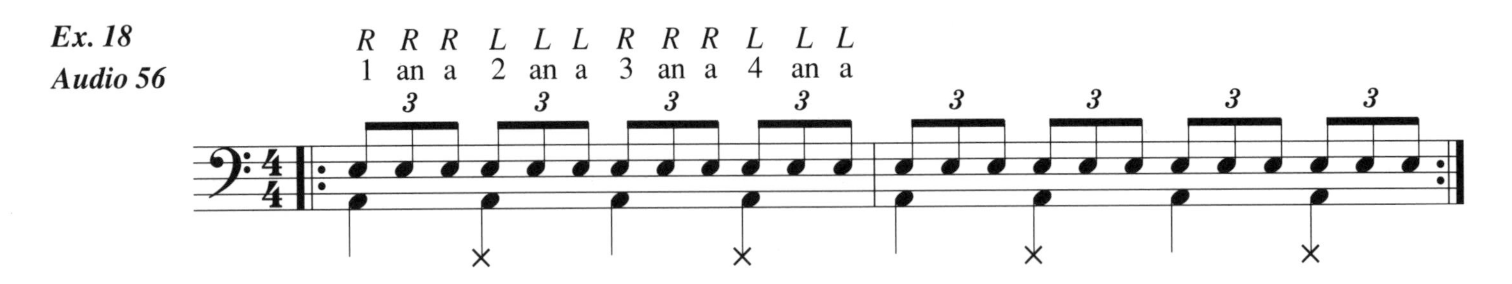

Exercise 19 Audio Track no. 57

In exercise 19 we play eighth note triplets on the ride cymbal with the right hand. The snare which is played with your left hand falls on beats 2 and 4. The bass and hi-hat play the same as the previous exercise.

Ex. 19
Audio 57

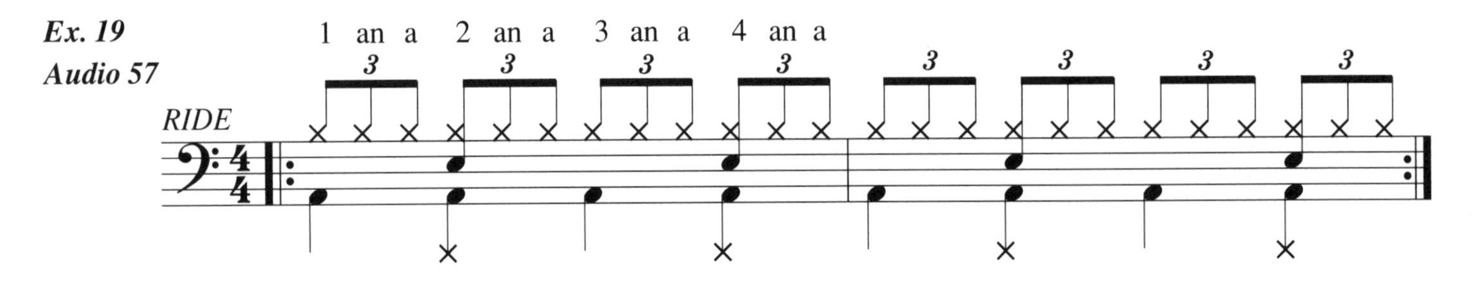

Practise these exercises at different tempos, from 35 bpm to 80 bpm.

TRIPLET RHYTHMS WITH BASS DRUM VARIATIONS

Exercise 20 Audio Track nos 58–61

In exercise 20 we have four bass drum variations using the eighth note triplet cymbal rhythm. The snare plays on beats 2 and 4 while the bass drum plays a different pattern in each exercise.

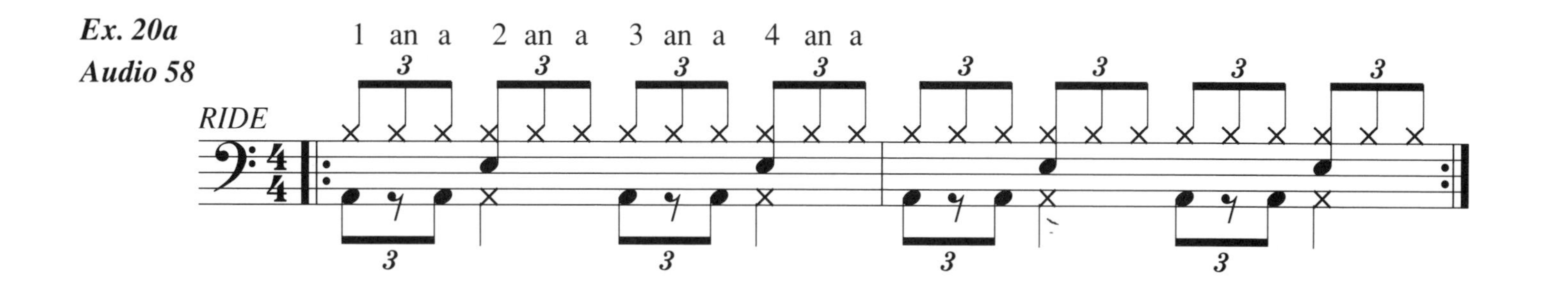

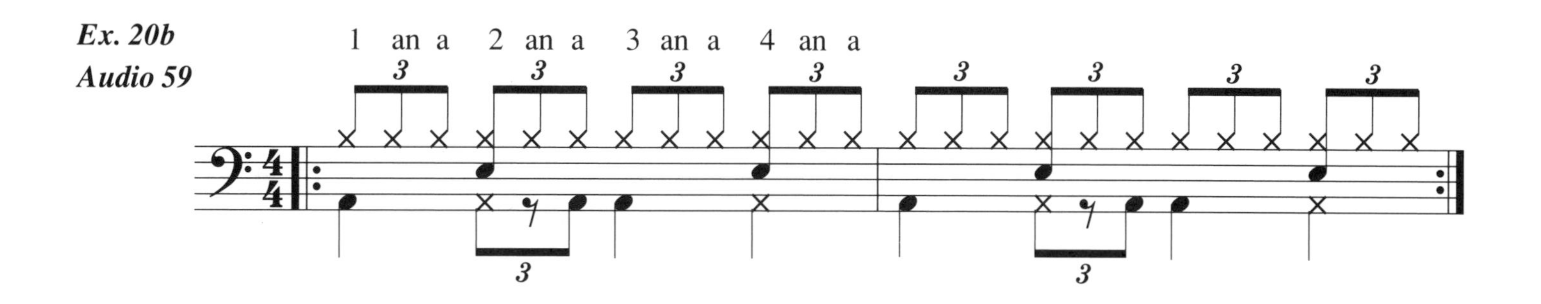

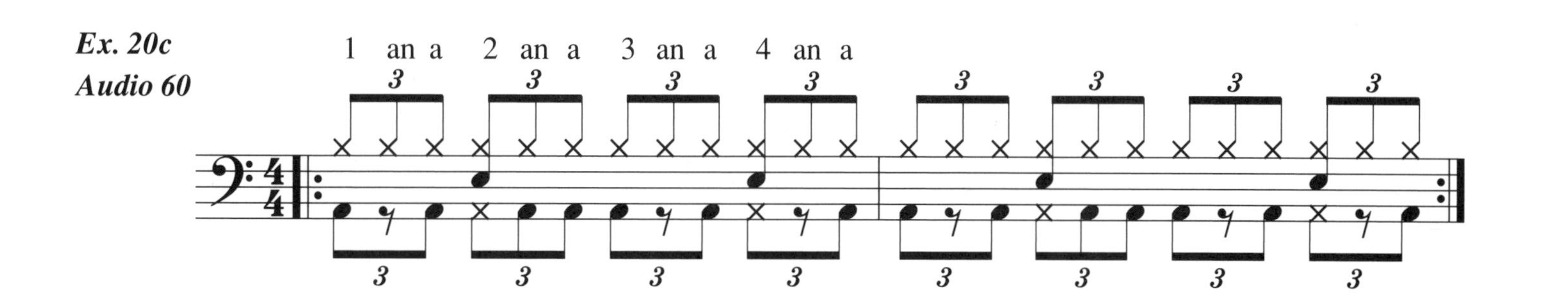

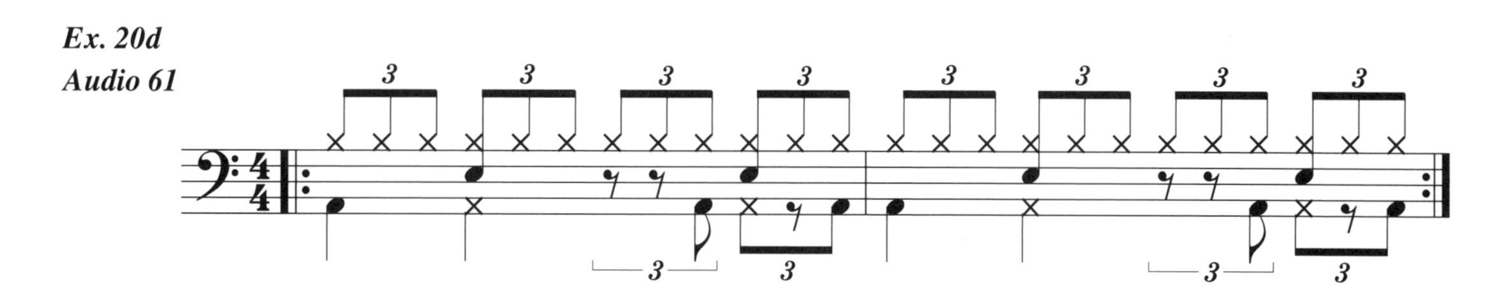

For extra practice play the ride cymbal pattern on the closed hi-hat. Practise these rhythms at different tempos, from 35 bpm to 80 bpm.

TRIPLET RHYTHMS WITH SNARE AND BASS DRUM VARIATIONS

Exercise 21 Audio Track nos 62–65

In exercise 21 we have four more variations on the eighth note triplet rhythm. This time we have different snare and bass drum patterns combined.

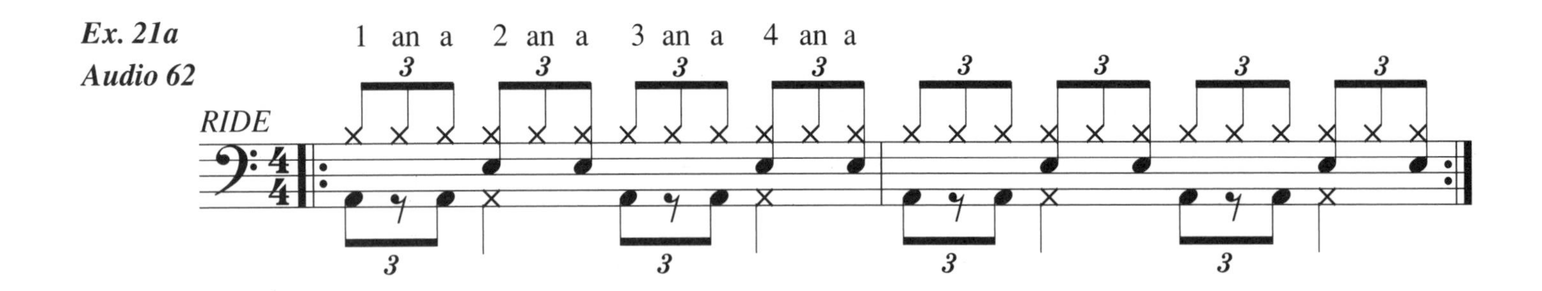

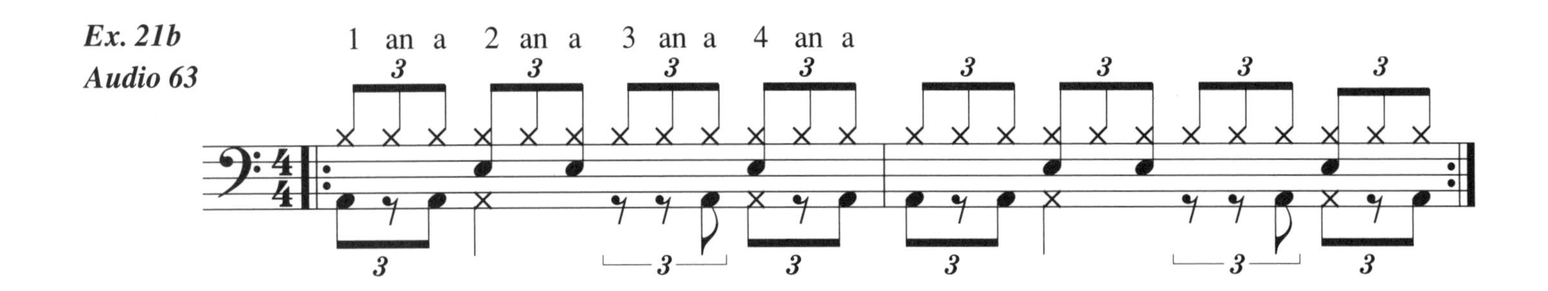

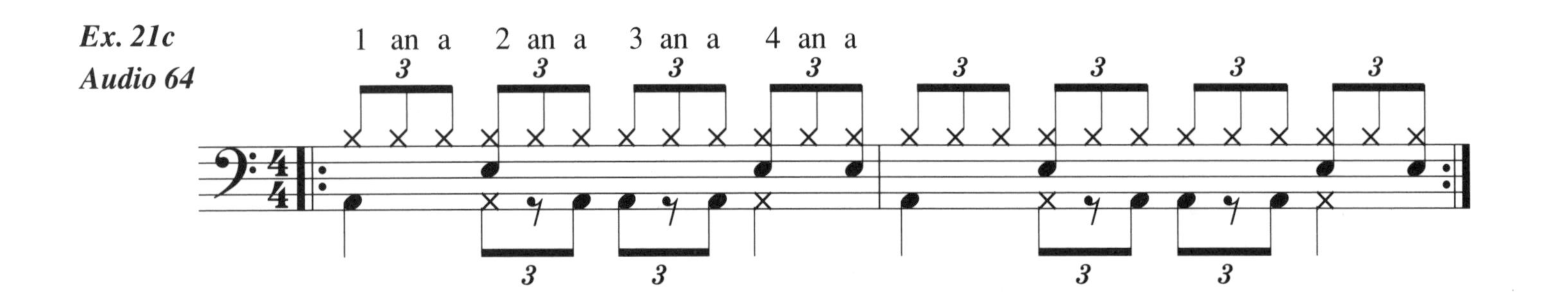

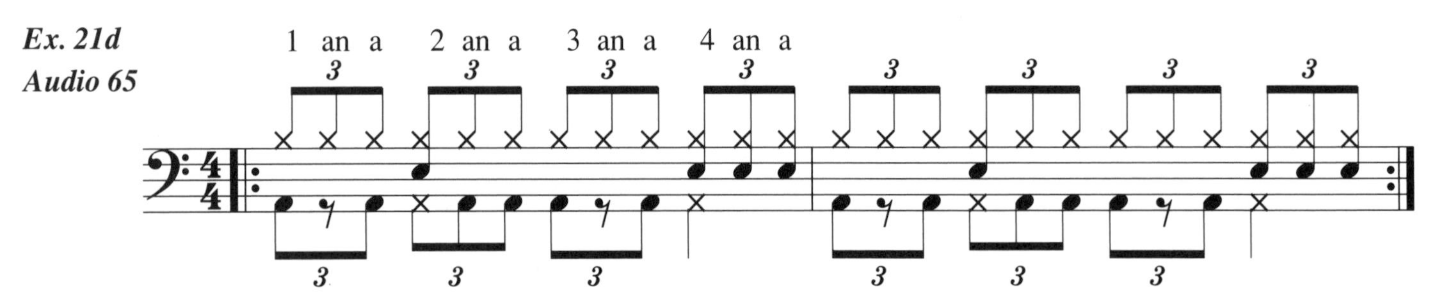

For extra practice play through exercise 21a to 21d without stopping.
For extra practice play the ride cymbal pattern on the closed hi-hat.
Practise these rhythms at different tempos, from 35 bpm to 80 bpm.

USING TRIPLET RHYTHMS (FOR SLOW TEMPOS)

Exercise 22 Audio Track nos 66 and 67

Exercise 22 is written in $\frac{4}{4}$ and is constructed of three, four bar sections (A, B, C,).

In PART A we play a slow triplet rhythm for four bars as practised in exercise 20b.

In PART B we move onto the ride cymbal and play the rhythm as practised in exercise 21c.

In PART C we play the rhythm as practised in exercise 21b for two bars and the rhythm as practised in exercise 21c for two bars.

The rhythms in exercise 22 can also be written in $\frac{12}{8}$ (as shown below).

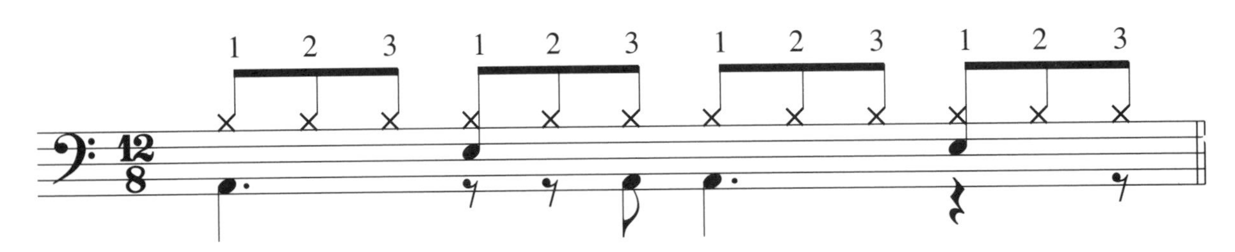

When written in $\frac{12}{8}$ the cymbal pattern is read as twelve quavers to a bar as opposed to four groups of triplets (as shown in the previous examples in this chapter). This could be counted 1, 2, 3, 4, 5, 6, 7, 8, 9, 10, 11, 12 etc., but to make it easier divide the count into four groups of three (4 x 3 = 12) as shown in the example above.

For a good example of the rhythms used in exercises 19–22 listen to METALLICA "Nothing Else Matters", BON JOVI "Bed of Roses", SOUNDGARDEN "Power Trip" and LED ZEPPELIN "Since I've Been Loving You".

Lars Ulrich, Metallica (LFI)

HEAVY METAL SHUFFLE RHYTHMS

Exercise 23 Audio Track no. 68

A shuffle rhythm is created by replacing the second eighth note of a triplet with a rest, as shown in exercise 23.

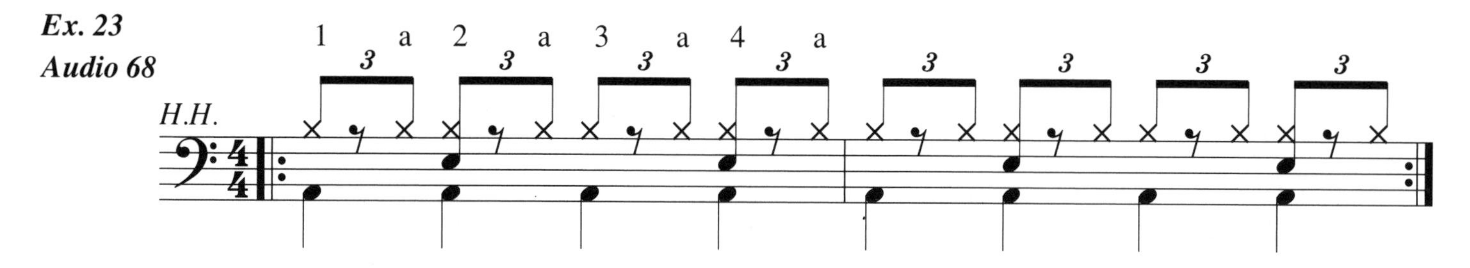

Exercise 24 Audio Track no. 69

In exercise 24 we have a shuffle rhythm with a different bass drum pattern.

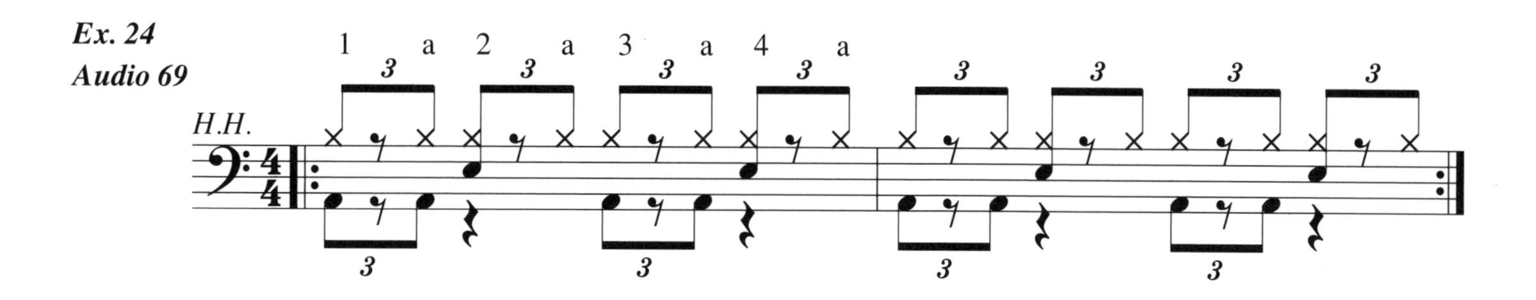

Practise these rhythms at different tempos, from 60 bpm to 130 bpm.

HEAVY METAL SHUFFLE RHYTHMS WITH BASS DRUM VARIATIONS

Exercise 25 Audio Track nos 70–73

In exercise 25 we have four more shuffle rhythms with bass drum variations. Make sure you give the eighth note rest its full value when counting.

Ex. 25a
Audio 70

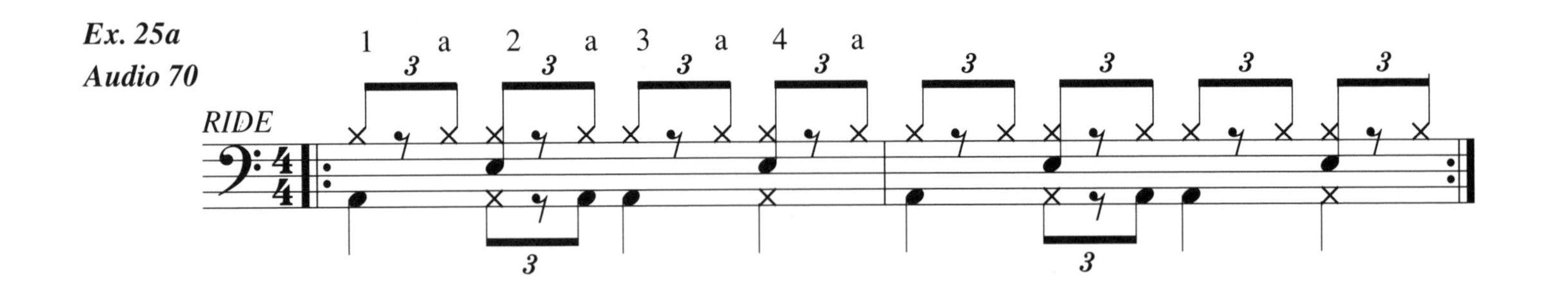

Ex. 25b
Audio 71

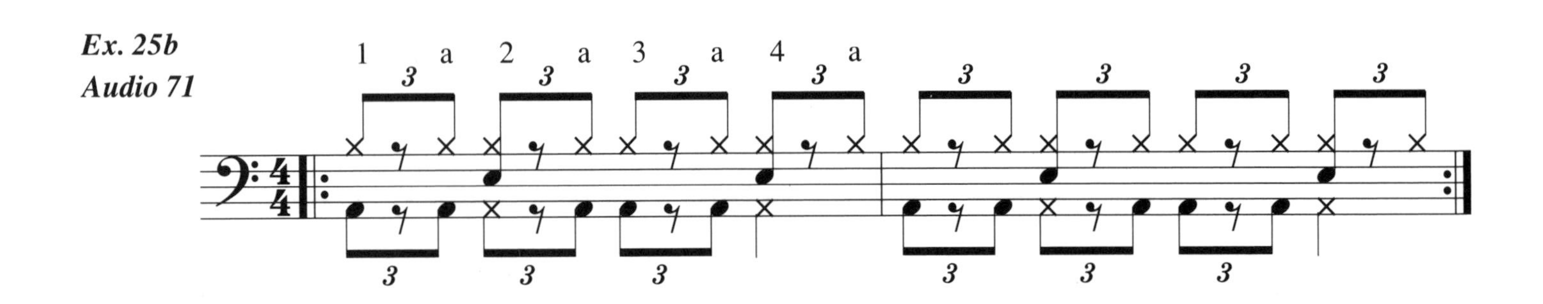

Ex. 25c
Audio 72

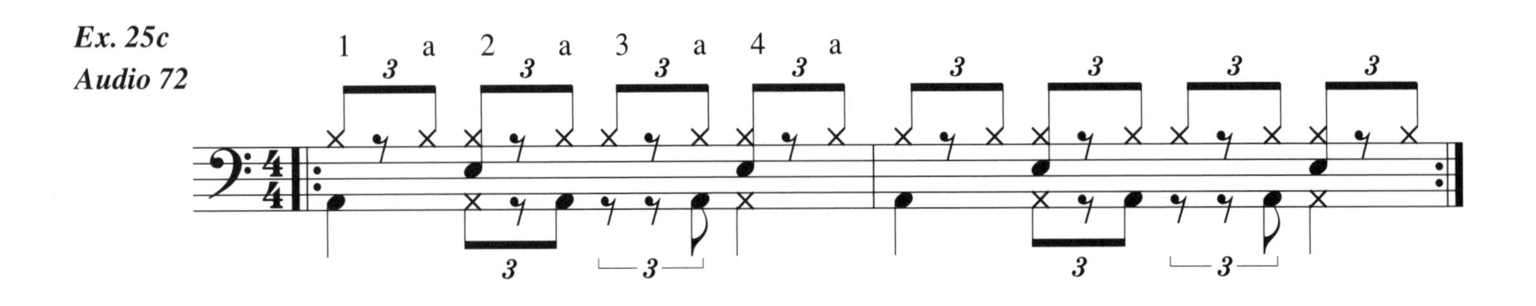

Ex. 25d
Audio 73

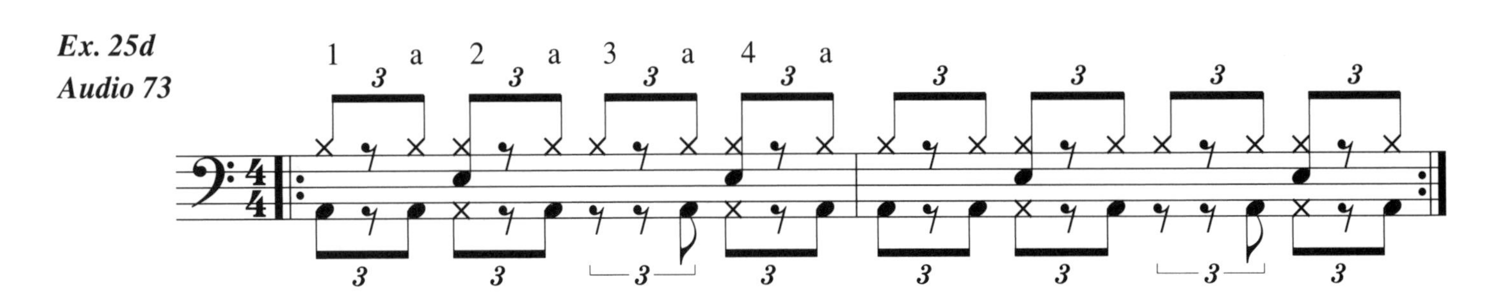

For extra practice play all the above ride cymbal rhythms on the closed hi-hat.
Practise these rhythms at different tempos, from 60 bpm to 130 bpm.

HEAVY METAL SHUFFLE RHYTHMS WITH SNARE AND BASS DRUM VARIATIONS

Exercise 26 Audio Track nos 74–77

In exercise 26 we have four more shuffle rhythms with different snare and bass drum variations. In exercise 26c the snare plays only on beat 3, and in exercise 26d on beat 4. This gives both these rhythms a half time feel.

Ex. 26a
Audio 74

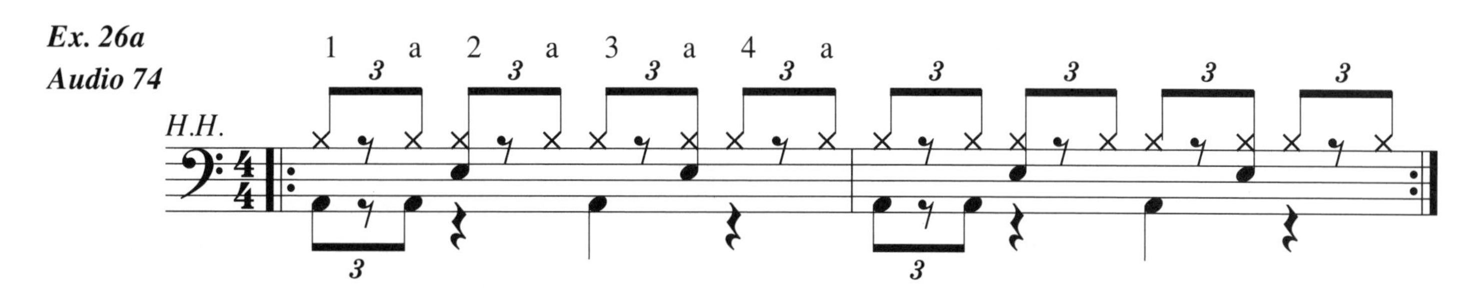

Ex. 26b
Audio 75

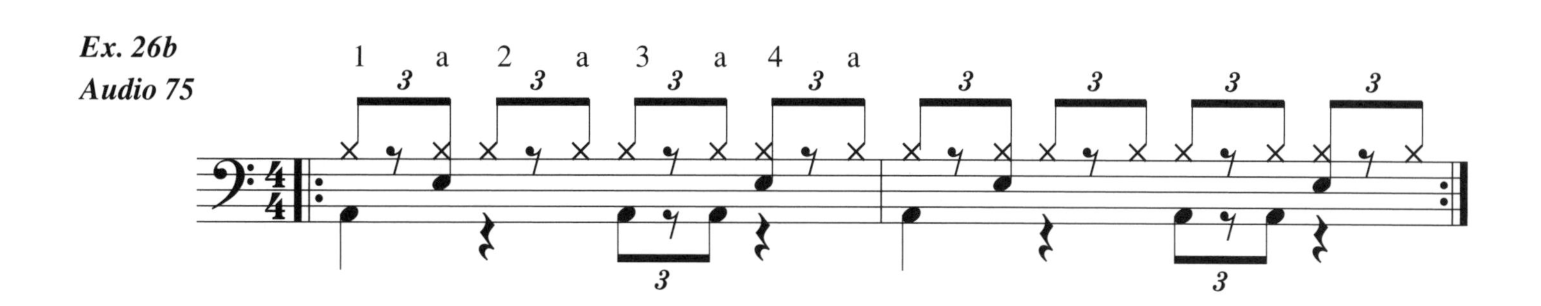

Ex. 26c
Audio 76

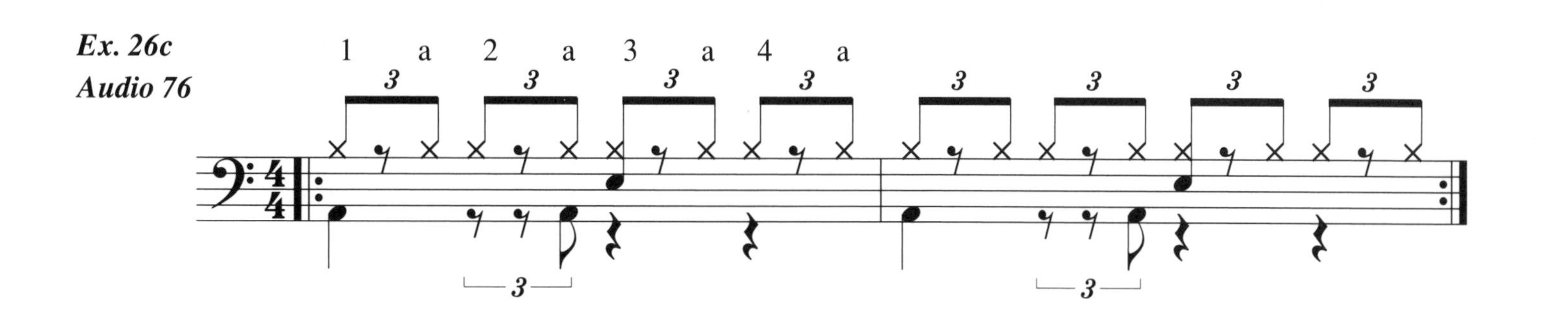

Ex. 26d
Audio 77

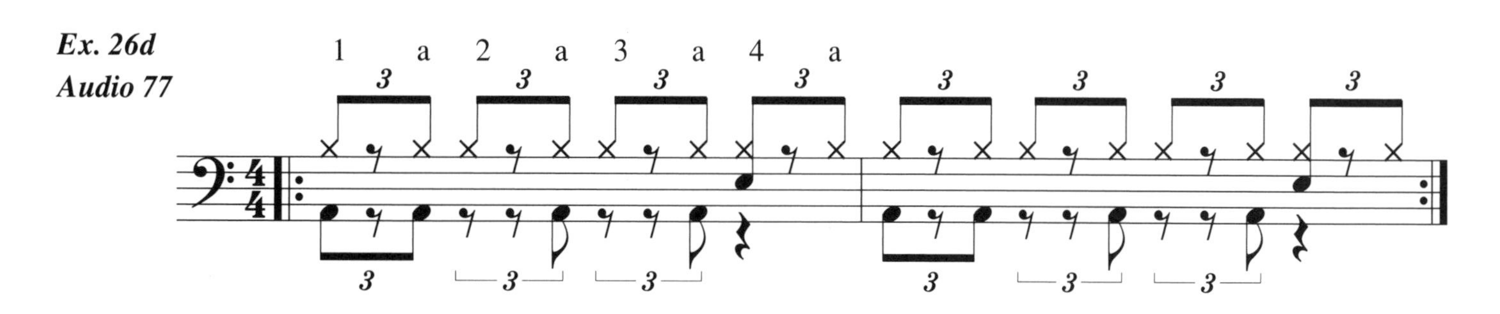

For extra practice play all the above closed hi-hat cymbal patterns on the ride cymbal. Practise these rhythms at different tempos, from 60 bpm to 130 bpm.

HEAVY METAL SHUFFLE RHYTHMS AND TRIPLET FILLS

Exercise 27 Audio Track no. 78

Exercise 27 is a two bar pattern. In bar 1 we have a shuffle rhythm, and in bar 2 a one bar triplet drum fill played on the snare using single stroke sticking (R L R L etc.). The bass drum plays an even four quarter note beats to the bar throughout, with the hi-hat falling on beats 2 and 4.

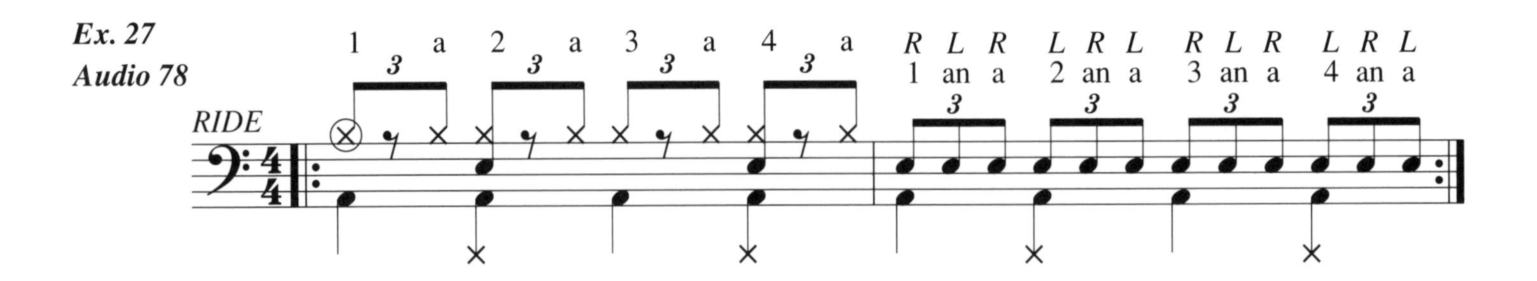

Exercise 28 Audio Track no. 79

In exercise 28 we have a variation on the triplet drum fill. On beats 2 and 4 the second eighth note of each triplet has been replaced with an eighth note rest.

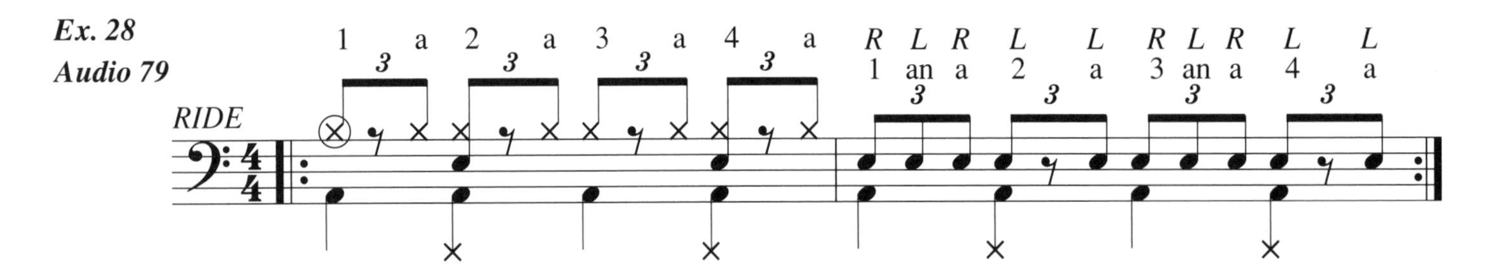

Note the crash cymbal on beat one in exercises 27 and 28.
Practise these rhythms at different tempos, from 70 bpm to 130 bpm.

HEAVY METAL SHUFFLE RHYTHMS AND TRIPLET FILLS (CONTINUED)

Exercise 29 Audio Track no. 80

In exercise 29 and 30 we have two more variations on the triplet drum fill.

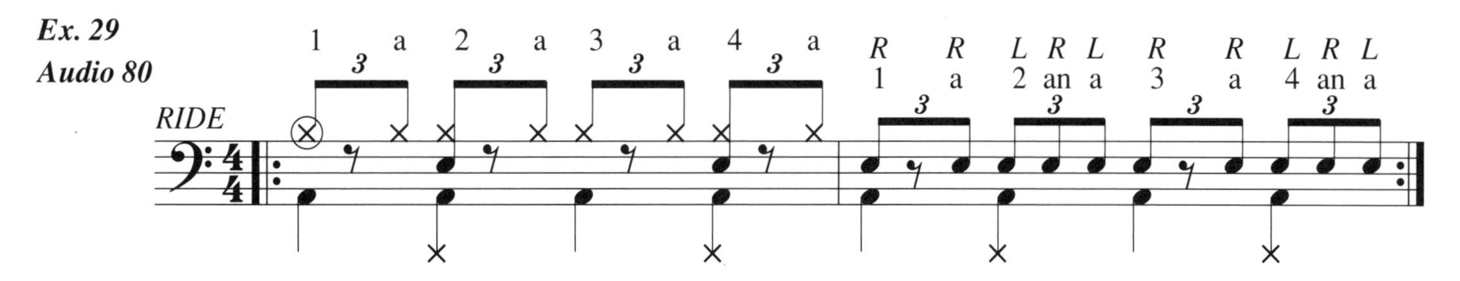

Exercise 30 Audio track no. 81

Try playing the cymbal pattern on the ride, the first time through. Then play the cymbal pattern on the closed hi-hat. Keep alternating between the ride and hi-hat. Be careful not to speed up or slow down.

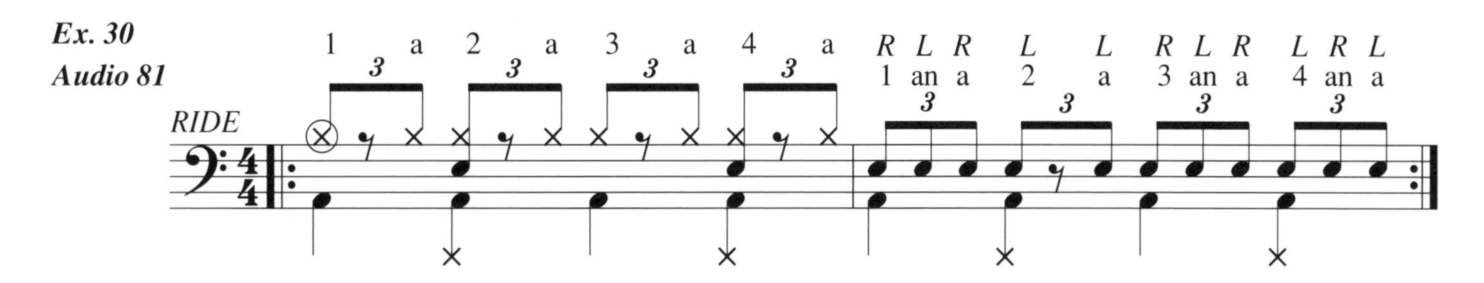

For extra practice in exercises 27, 28, 29 and 30 play THREE bars of rhythm before playing the one bar drum fill, this turns these exercises into four bar patterns.
For extra practice, substitute the rhythm bars of exercises 29 and 30 with those of 25 and 26.
Practise these rhythms at different tempos, from 70 bpm to 130 bpm.

HEAVY METAL SHUFFLE RHYTHMS USING QUARTER NOTE HI-HAT PATTERNS

Exercise 31 Audio Track no. 82

In exercise 31 we have a shuffle rhythm with the closed hi-hat playing a straight quarter note pattern. This produces a much heavier feel to the rhythm than the previous shuffles.

Ex. 31
Audio 82

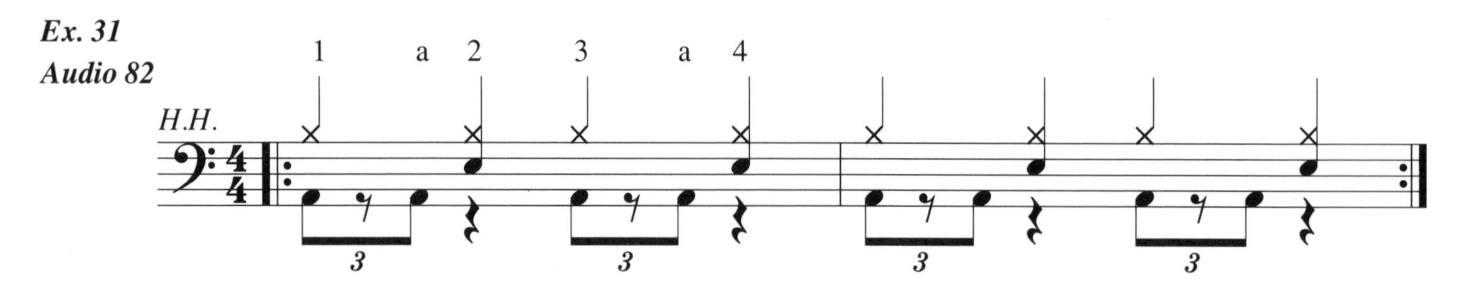

Exercise 32 Audio Track no. 83

In exercise 32 we have a different bass drum pattern. Make sure your closed hi-hat pattern plays a steady quarter note rhythm and does not follow the bass drum pattern.

Ex. 32
Audio 83

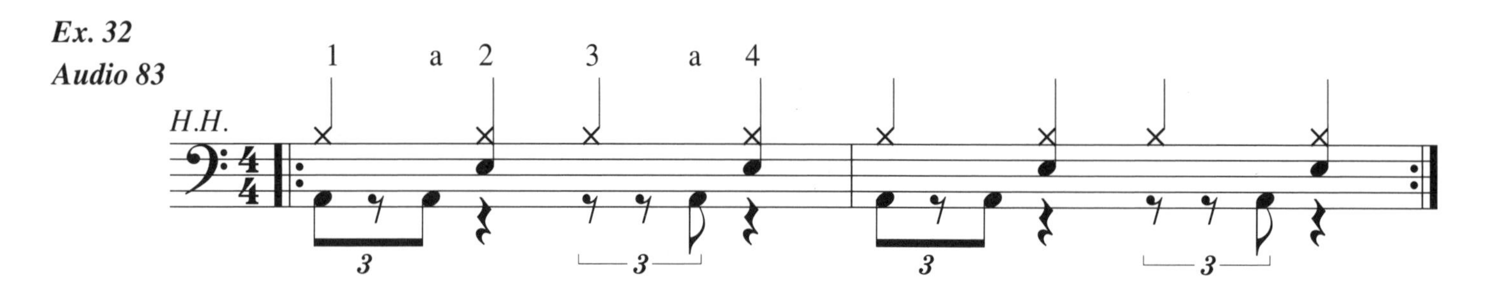

Practise these rhythms at different tempos, from 90 bpm to 140 bpm.

HEAVY METAL SHUFFLE RHYTHMS USING QUARTER NOTE HI-HAT PATTERNS (CONTINUED)

Exercise 33 Audio Track nos 84–87

In exercise 33 we have four more bass drum variations. In exercise 33c the snare only plays on beat 3 and 33d on beat 4. Both these rhythms have a half time feel.

For extra practice play all the hi-hat patterns on the bell of the ride cymbal or cowbell.
For extra practice combine the one bar triplet drum fills from exercises 27, 28, 29 and 30 with these rhythms (forming four bar patterns) as described on page 41.
Practise these rhythms at different tempos, from 90 bpm to 140 bpm.

USING SHUFFLE RHYTHMS AND TRIPLET FILLS

Exercise 34 Audio Track nos 88 and 89

Having practised all the rhythms in chapter 4 you will now be able to feel the difference between a STRAIGHT EIGHT or quarter note rhythm (as shown in exercises 1–16, chapter 2) and an eighth or quarter note SHUFFLE or TRIPLET rhythm (as shown in exercises 18–34, chapter 4).

Generally when playing a shuffle rhythm you would use a triplet drum fill, and when playing a straight eight rock rhythm a straight eight or sixteenth note fill.*

Exercise 34 is written in $\frac{4}{4}$ and is constructed of three sixteen bar sections (A, B, C).

In PART A we play an eighth note shuffle rhythm (on the hi-hat) as practised in exercise 23.

In PART B we move to the ride cymbal and play the rhythm as practised in exercise 25b. Note the triplet fill (as played in exercise 27) in bar thirty two.

In PART C we play a shuffle rhythm with a quarter note pattern played on the bell of the ride cymbal as practised in exercise 31.

For a good example of the rhythms used in exercises 23–34 listen to DEEP PURPLE "Black Night", "Demon's Eye", VAN HALEN "When It's Love" and METALLICA "Don't Tread On Me".

Alex Van Halen (LFI)

*There are no strict rules regarding the type of fill you can play with any rhythm, this is only a general guide.

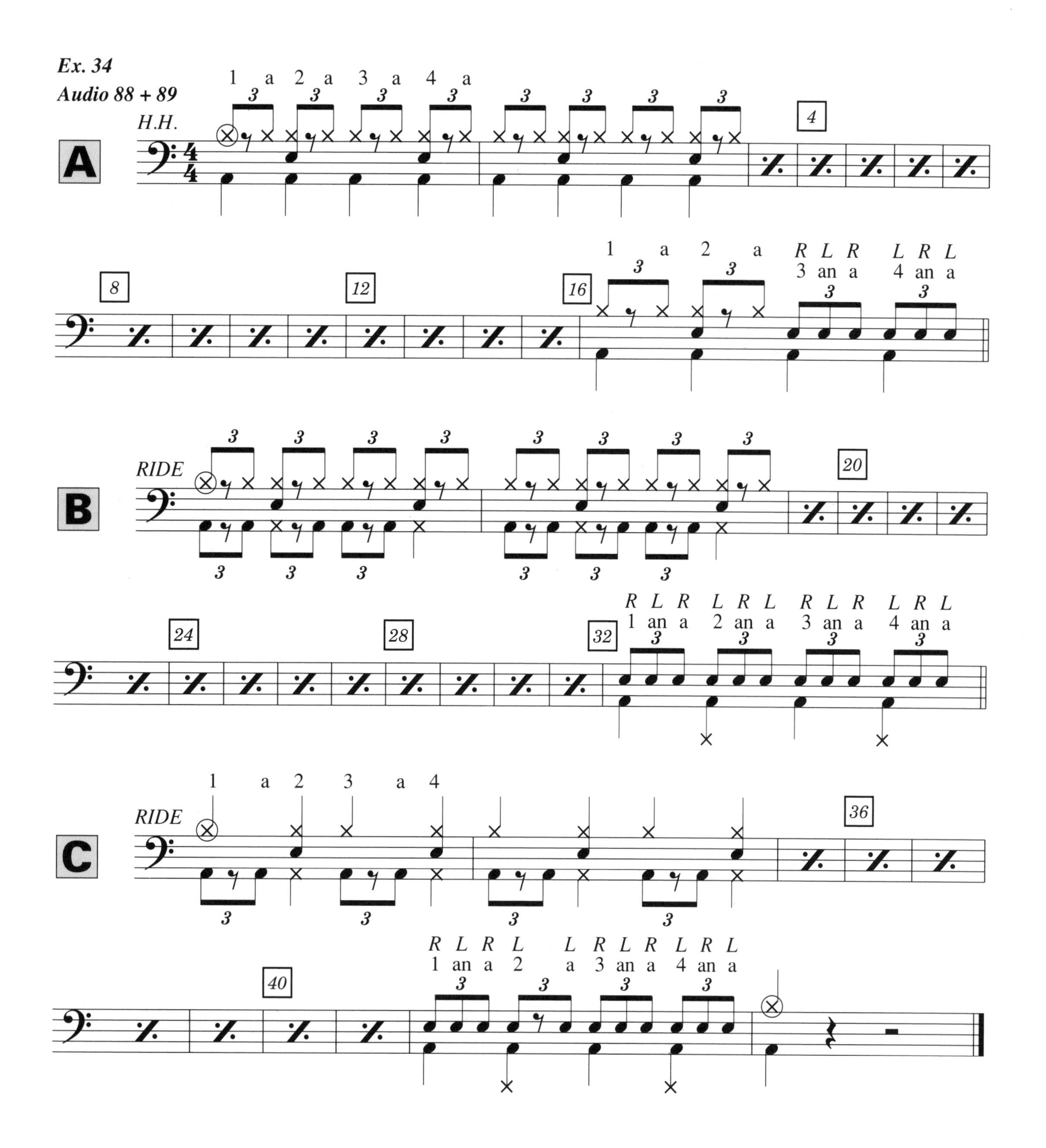
Ex. 34
Audio 88 + 89
A
H.H.
1 a 2 a 3 a 4 a
4
8
12
16
1 a 2 a
R L R L R L
3 an a 4 an a
B
RIDE
20
24
28
32
R L R L R L R L R L R L
1 an a 2 an a 3 an a 4 an a
C
RIDE
1 a 2 3 a 4
36
40
R L R L L R L R L R L
1 an a 2 a 3 an a 4 an a

Chapter 5

DRUM FILLS AROUND THE KIT (STARTING ON DIFFERENT BEATS)

Exercise 35 Audio Track no. 90

In exercise 35 we have a bar of rhythm, followed by a one bar drum fill which moves between the snare and top-tom then down to the floor tom. As you go around the kit make sure all the beats are even in tempo and volume.

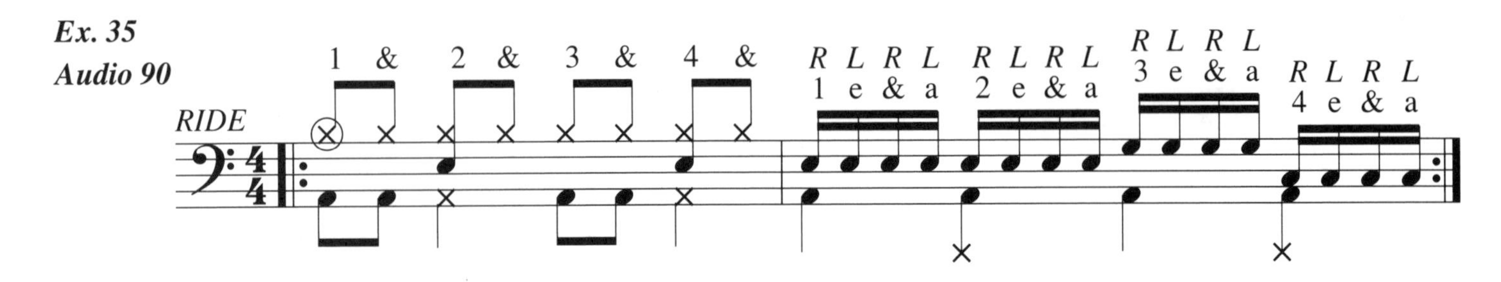

Exercise 36 Audio Track no. 91

In exercise 36 the drum fill starts on beat two and moves around the kit from the snare to the top-tom then down to the floor tom.

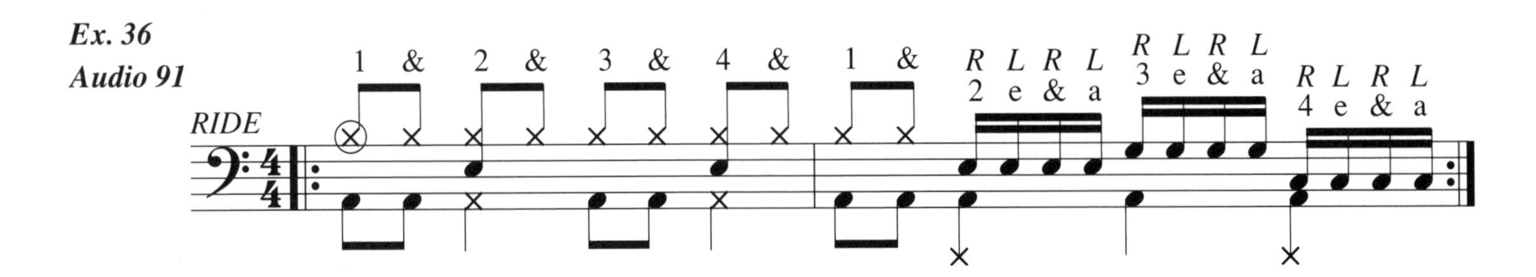

Note the crash cymbal is played with your right hand in bar one, on beat one, in both the above exercises.

For extra practice substitute the above rhythms for any of the rhythms as practised in exercises 2–9.

Practise these exercises at different tempos, from 70 bpm to 130 bpm.

Exercise 37 Audio Track no. 92

In exercise 37 the drum fill is over two beats and starts on beat three.

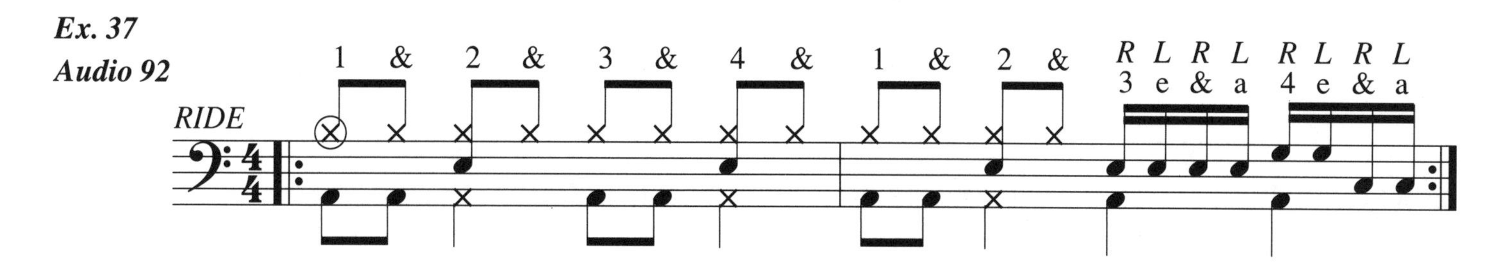

Exercise 38 Audio Track no. 93

In exercise 38 we have a one beat fill starting on beat four.

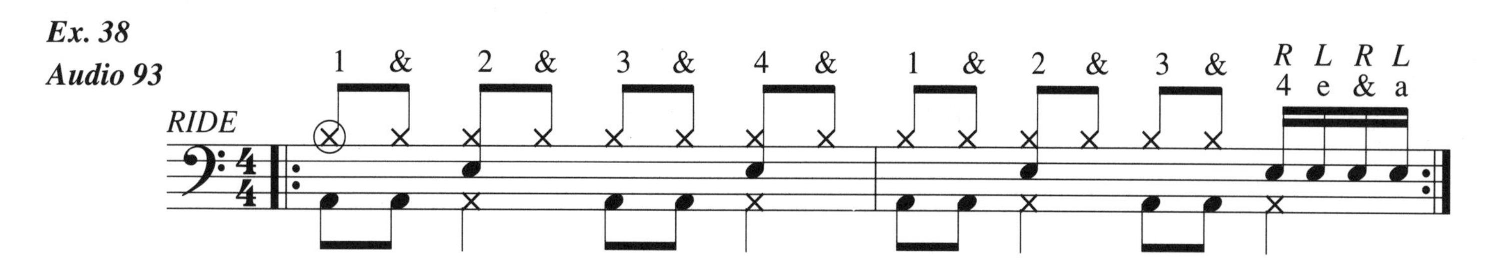

Note in exercise 37 although you play eight sixteenth note beats for the snare fill, it is equal to two quarter note beats, so it is referred to as a two beat fill.

In exercise 38 you play four sixteenth notes for the snare fill which is equal to one quarter note beat, so it is referred to as a one beat fill.
For extra practice play the ride cymbal pattern on the closed hi-hat.
For extra practice in exercises 35, 36, 37 and 38 play three bars of rhythm before the bar with a fill. This will turn these exercises into four bar patterns.
Practise these exercises at different tempos, from 70 bpm to 130 bpm.

USING DRUM FILLS AROUND THE KIT

Exercise 39 Audio Track nos 94 and 95

When playing a drum fill it is important not to lose the tempo or groove of the song you are playing. First, decide how many beats the fill will cover and on which beat the fill will start. e.g., a two beat fill (in a bar of $\frac{4}{4}$) will usually start on beat three, a one beat fill will usually start on beat four.

Often a fill for one or two beats will flow better than a fill for a whole bar. Remember that you are not there to show what you can do to the detriment of the other musicians you are playing with.

The most in demand drummers are those that listen to the other players, keep good time* and do not over play.

Exercise 39 is written in $\frac{4}{4}$ and consists of two eight bar sections, A and B (which are repeated) with a drum fill in every eighth bar. The first fill is over four beats and the second fill is over two beats. Try to create as many different fills as you can.

When playing fills keep a steady quarter note pattern on the bass drum (playing on beats 1, 2, 3 ,4). This will help keep your fills in time and add some depth of sound.

For extra practice substitute the rhythm bars of exercise 39 with those of exercises 3–10.

---

* Keeping good time means not slowing down or speeding up but keeping a rock solid tempo throughout the song.

Exercise 39 Audio Track nos 94–95

Chapter 6

DRUM RUDIMENTS
THE DOUBLE STROKE ROLL

Exercise 40 Audio Track no. 96

In exercise 40 there are no bar lines or time signature. This is because unlike all the previous exercises in this book you start the double stroke roll very slowly (open) playing two beats with each hand e.g. R R L L etc. and gradually increase the speed (close) then gradually and EVENLY decrease the speed bringing you back to your starting point.

When practising the double stroke roll let each beat bounce back off the drum head up to the same height and make sure every beat is played with an equal amount of volume (especially the second beat of every double). As soon as you feel yourself becoming tense or uneven start to gradually slow the roll down.

For extra practise play the double stroke roll starting with your left hand e.g., L L R R etc.

I have left this exercise until the end of Part 1 because drum rudiments are among some of the more difficult aspects of drumming to accomplish. However, in order to progress and become more proficient you should devote some time at the start of each practice session to the Double Stroke roll.

Exercise 41 Audio Track nos 97 and 98

Exercise 41 is written in $\frac{4}{4}$ and consists of three parts, A, B and C.

In PART A we have a shuffle rhythm using a heavy quarter note pattern on the closed hi-hat as practised in chapter 4 exercises 31–33.

Note the four different two beat triplet fills in bars 5, 9, 13 and 17.

In PART B the closed hi-hat pattern changes to a straight eighth note rhythm with the snare falling on beat three, this gives a half time feel to the rhythm as practised in chapter 2 exercise 5d.

In PART C we have a heavy rock rhythm using a quarter note pattern played on the bell of the ride cymbal as practised in chapter 2 exercise 8.

Note the eight bar repeat section in PART C.

John Bonham, Led Zeppelin (LFI)

Ex. 41
Audio 97 + 98
A
H.H.
1 2 3 4
1 a 2 3 a 4
1 a 2 a 3 a 4
R L R L R L
1 an a 2 an a 3 4
R L R L R L
R L R L R L
R L R L R L
B
1 & 2 & 3 & 4 &

RL R
1 e &
R RL
2 &a
RL RL
3 e & a
RL RL
4 e & a
C
RIDE
1 & 2 3 & 4
1 & 2 & 3 & 4
1 & 2 & 3 4
2
2
R L R L R L
1 & 2 & 3 &
R L R L
4 e & a

SUMMARY

Having practised all the exercises in Part 1 you will now have gained a valuable understanding of reading and playing basic rock drum rhythms and fills.

If you have enjoyed working your way through Part 1, why not move on to Part 2 where among other things we will cover:

Syncopation
Sixteenth note bass drum and cymbal patterns
Drum intros and fills
Rhythms in different time signatures
Drum rudiments

and many more essential aspects of drumming.

How To Play
Rock Drums

Dave Zubraski

PART 2

Chapter 1

SYNCOPATION

Exercise 1 Audio Track no. 2

So far in all the previous rhythms (in Part 1) where we have used an eighth note ride cymbal or hi-hat pattern, the snare drum has fallen in time with one or more of the cymbal beats.
In exercise 1 we have a sixteenth snare drum note after beat three. This is called a syncopated beat because it falls between the cymbal beats and not with them.
(Note the snare drum also plays on beats 2 and 4).

Ex. 1
Audio 2

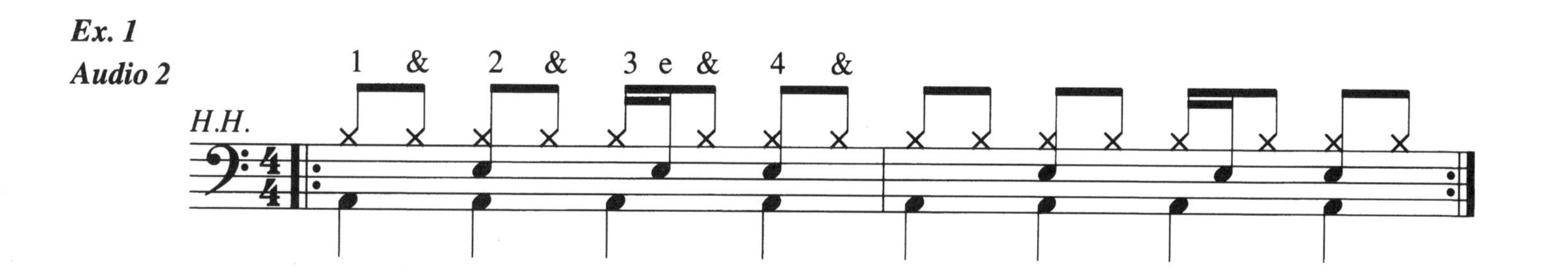

Exercise 2 Audio Track no. 3

In exercise 2 the syncopated snare beat is after beat one.
When playing these syncopated rhythms make sure the cymbal pattern maintains an even rhythm playing eighth notes.

Ex. 2
Audio 3

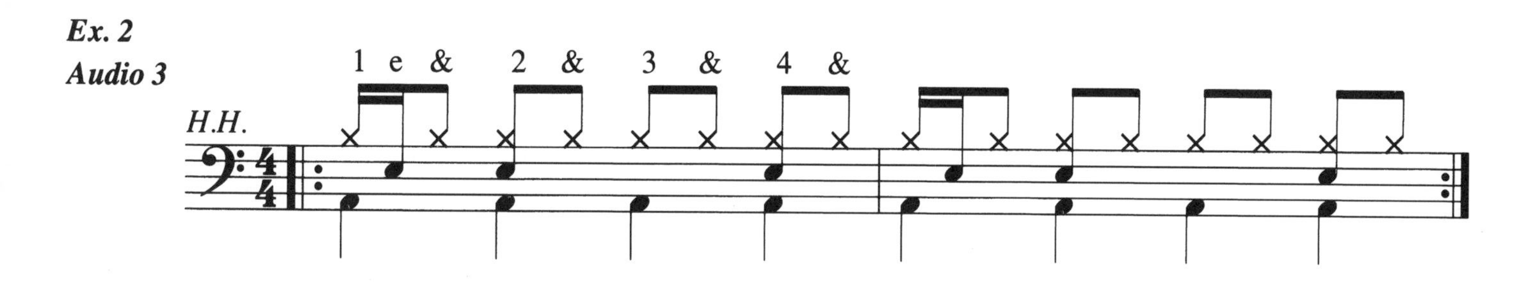

For extra practice play all the closed hi-hat patterns on the ride cymbal.
(When playing the ride, close the hi-hat on beats 2 and 4.)
Practice these rhythms at different tempos, from 80 bpm to 130 bpm.

HEAVY METAL SYNCOPATED SNARE DRUM RHYTHMS

Exercise 3 Audio Track nos 4–7

In exercise 3 we have four more syncopated snare patterns. The bass drum plays on beats 1 and 3 throughout.

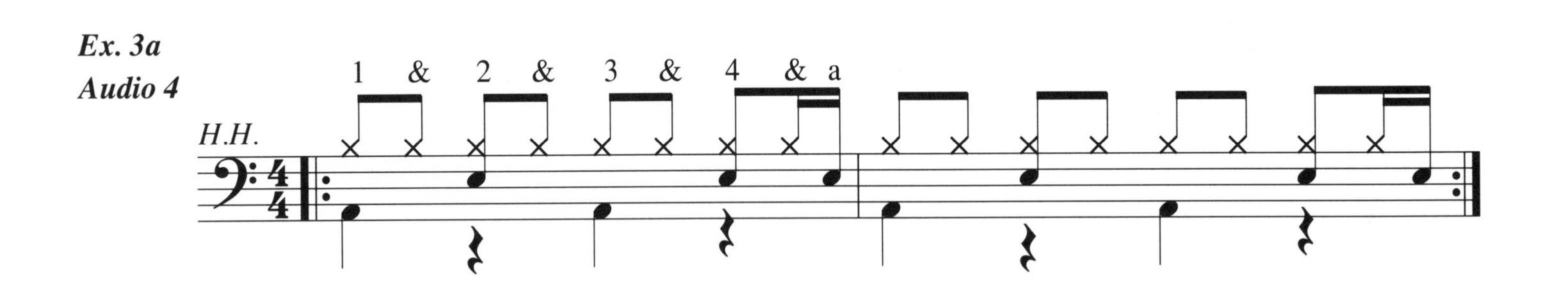

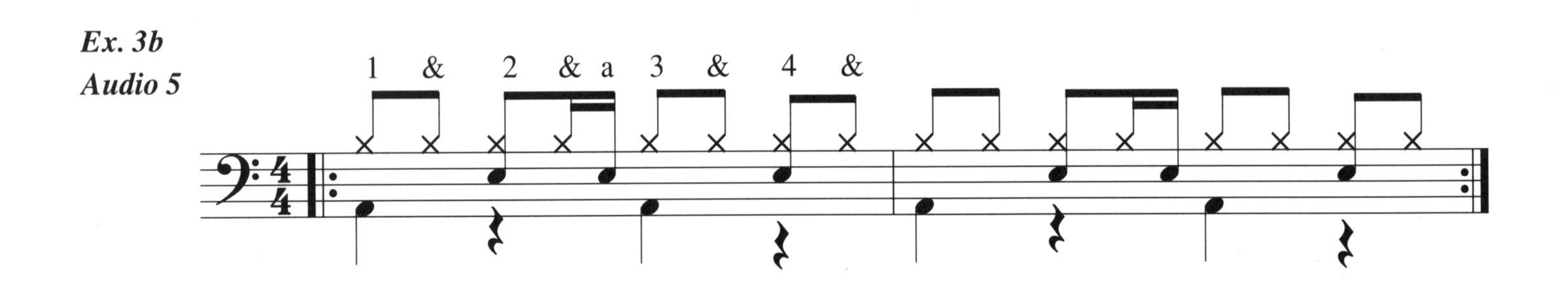

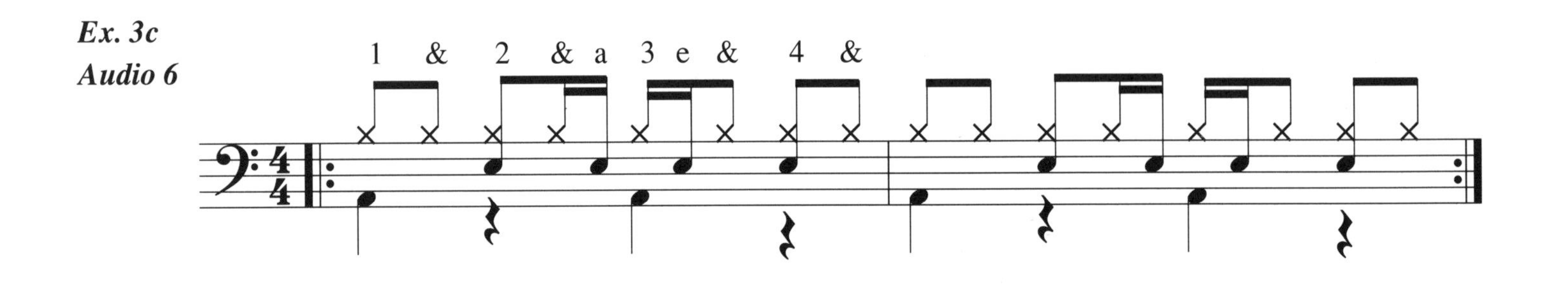

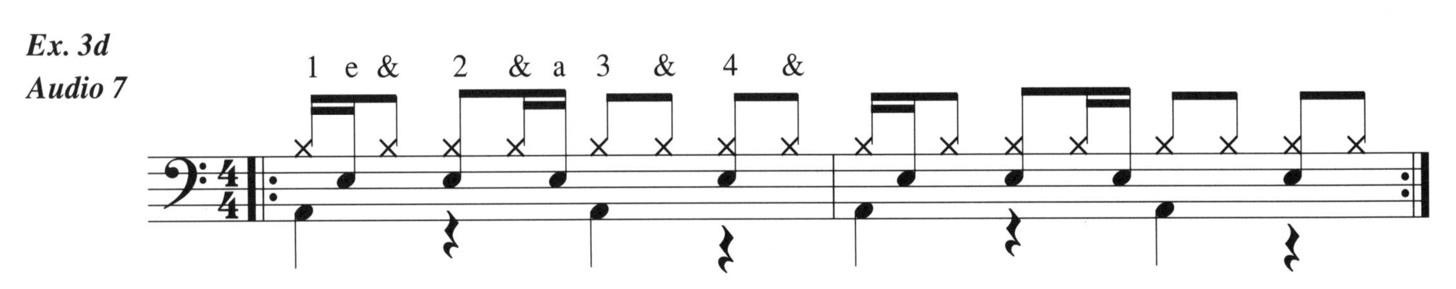

For extra practice alternate the cymbal rhythm between the closed hi-hat and ride, play four bars on each.
For extra practice play exercise 3a through to exercise 3d without stopping.
Practise these rhythms at different tempos, from 80 bpm to 130 bpm.

SYNCOPATED SNARE AND BASS DRUM RHYTHMS

Exercise 4 Audio Track nos 8–11

In exercise 4 we have four more variations of syncopated rhythms. This time the bass drum pattern changes in each exercise. The ride cymbal plays a constant eighth note pattern with the hi-hat falling on beats 2 and 4 throughout.

Ex. 4a
Audio 8

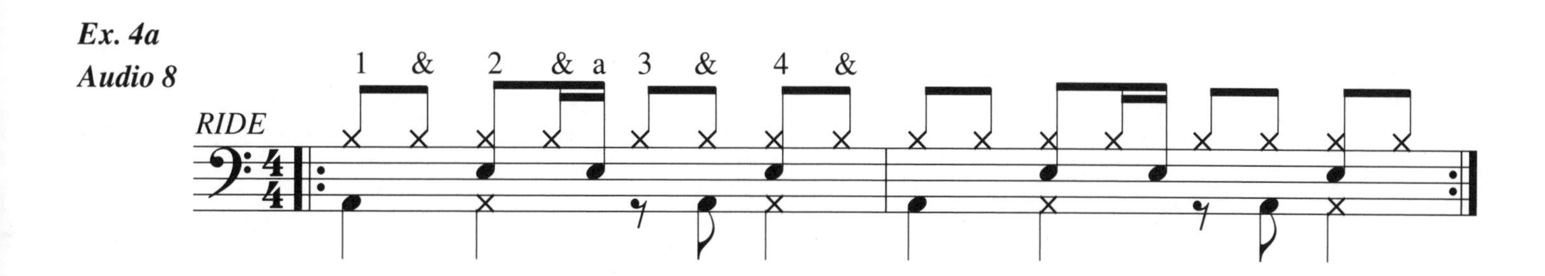

Ex. 4b
Audio 9

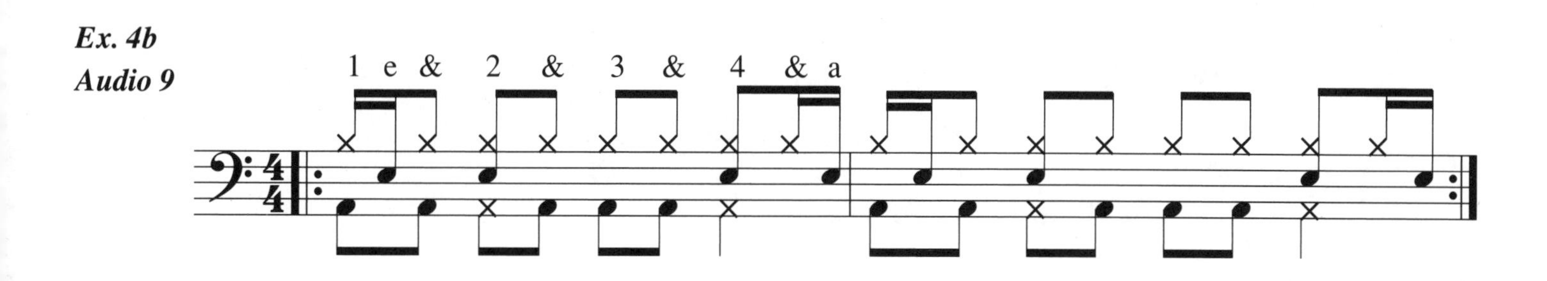

Ex. 4c
Audio 10

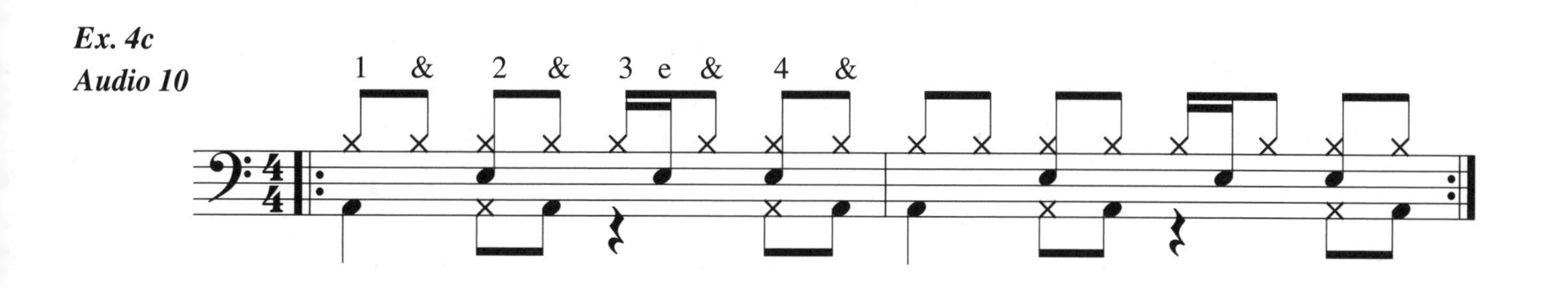

Ex. 4d
Audio 11

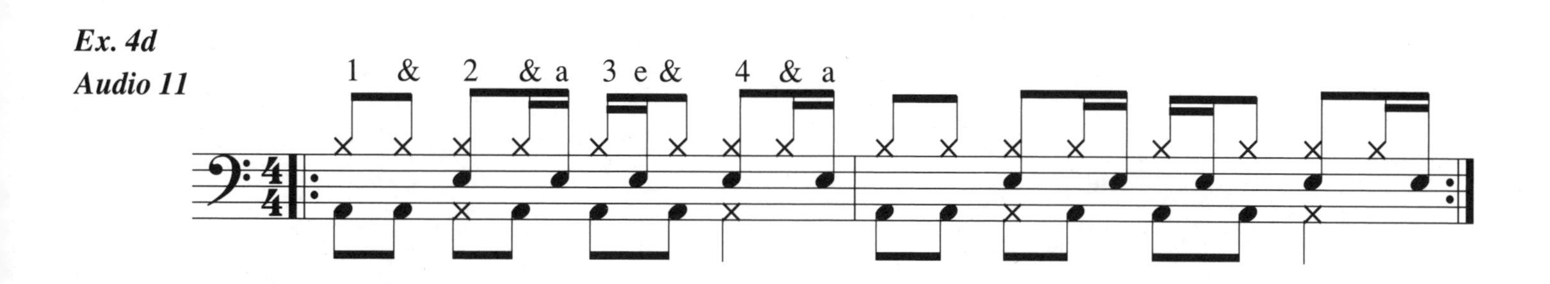

For extra practice play all the ride cymbal patterns on the closed hi-hat.
For extra practice play from exercise 8a through to exercise 8d without stopping.
Practise these rhythms at different tempos, from 80 bpm to 130 bpm.

USING SYNCOPATED RHYTHMS (IN TWO-BAR PATTERNS)

Exercise 5 Audio Track nos 12 and 13

Having practised all the exercises in this chapter you will have noticed that syncopated rhythms tend to feel busier than the previous rhythms we covered in Part 1. Although syncopated rhythms are exciting to play, be careful not to over-use them. If the drummer is too "busy", he will stop the music from "breathing". Always listen to, and leave room for, the other members of the band.

Exercise 5 is written in $\frac{4}{4}$ and consists of four parts (A,B,C,D).

In PART A we have a two-bar rhythm pattern. In the first bar we play the syncopated rhythm as practised in exercise 4a and in the second bar we play the same rhythm but without the syncopated snare beat. Note the repeat signs at the beginning and end of this part.

In PART B we have another two-bar pattern. In the first bar we play the syncopated rhythm as used in exercise 4d and in the second bar we play the same rhythm but again without the syncopated snare beats.

In PART C we move back onto the hi-hat and play the same two-bar rhythm as in part A.

In PART D we play the same two-bar rhythm as in part B for the last eight bars.

Note that the repeat signs in this exercise are different from the previous repeat signs we have used.

This repeat sign 𝄢 2 𝄏 means you repeat the previous TWO bars.

Ex.5 Audio 12 + 13

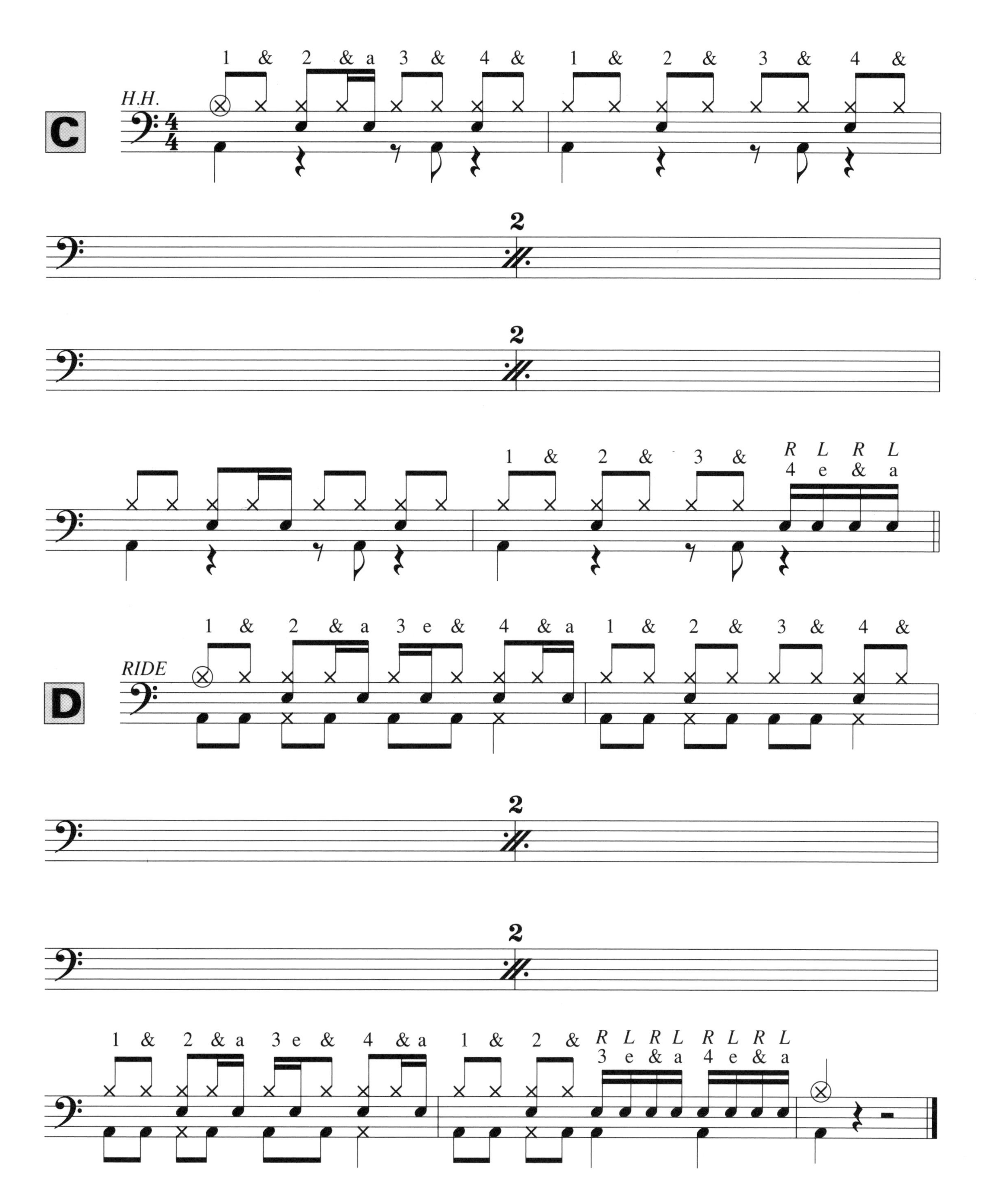

For some good examples of the type of rhythms used in this chapter listen to THE BLACK CROWES "Hard to Handle", PEARL JAM "Once", JIMI HENDRIX "Fire", and NIRVANA "Smells Like Teen Spirit".

Chapter 2

DOTTED NOTES AND RESTS

When a single dot is placed directly after a note, it increases the value or duration of that note by one half of its original value. This also applies to RESTS. Consequently, a DOTTED QUARTER NOTE is equal in duration to one quarter note plus one eighth note or its equivalent, as shown below.

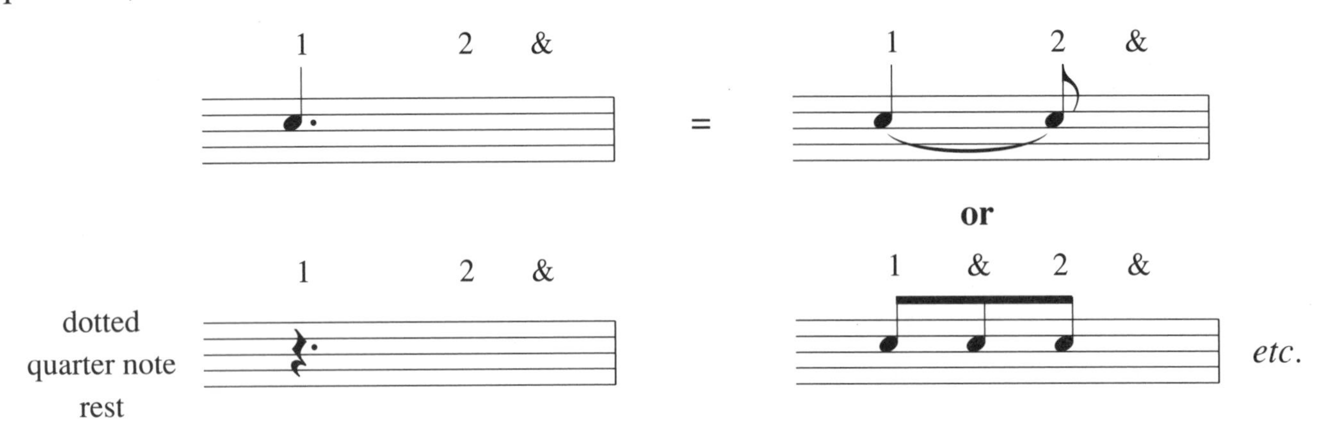

A DOTTED EIGHTH NOTE is equal in duration to one eighth note plus one sixteenth note or their equivalent, as shown below.

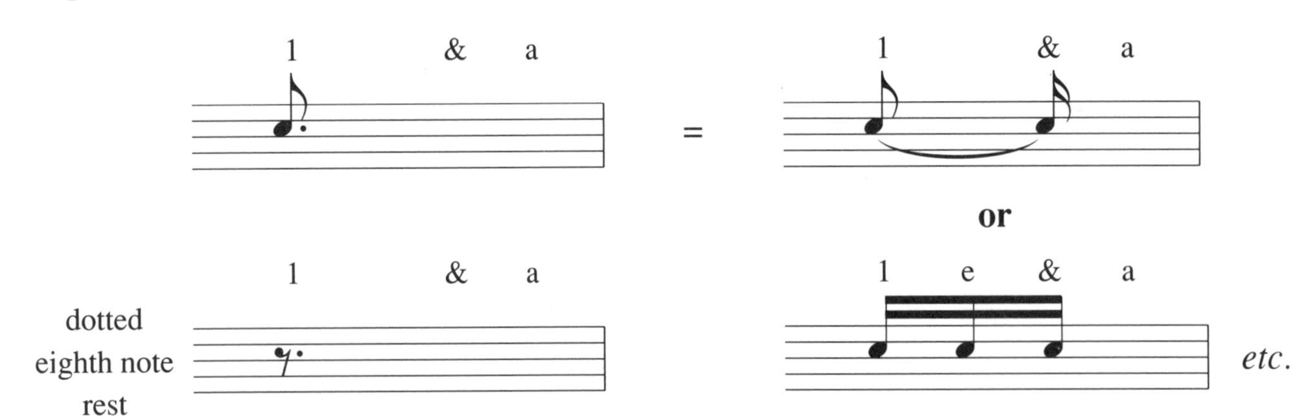

Exercise 6 Audio Track no. 14

In exercise 6 we have a rhythm with a dotted note bass drum pattern. Note the second bass drum beat falls between the eighth note hi-hat beats.

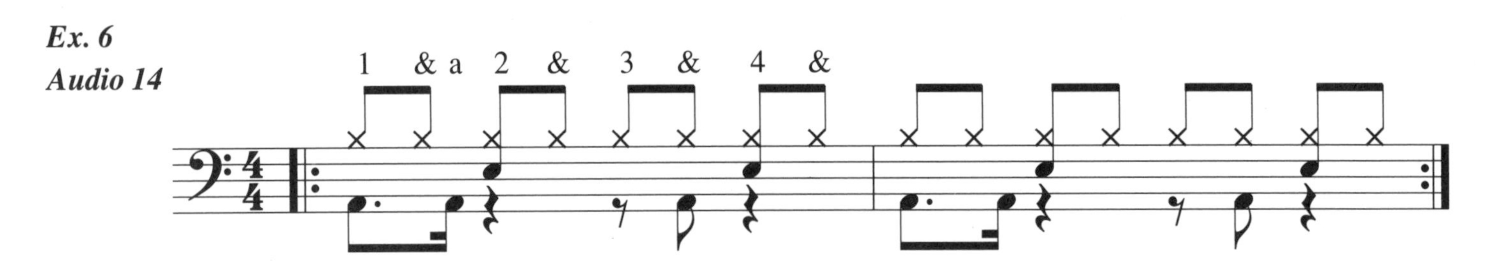

Practise this rhythm at different tempos, from 60 bpm to 120 bpm.

HEAVY METAL SIXTEENTH NOTE BASS DRUM PATTERNS

Exercise 7 Audio Track no. 15

In exercise 7 we have a sixteenth bass drum note before beat 3, this falls between the closed hi-hat cymbal beats. Note the dotted bass drum rest on beat 2.

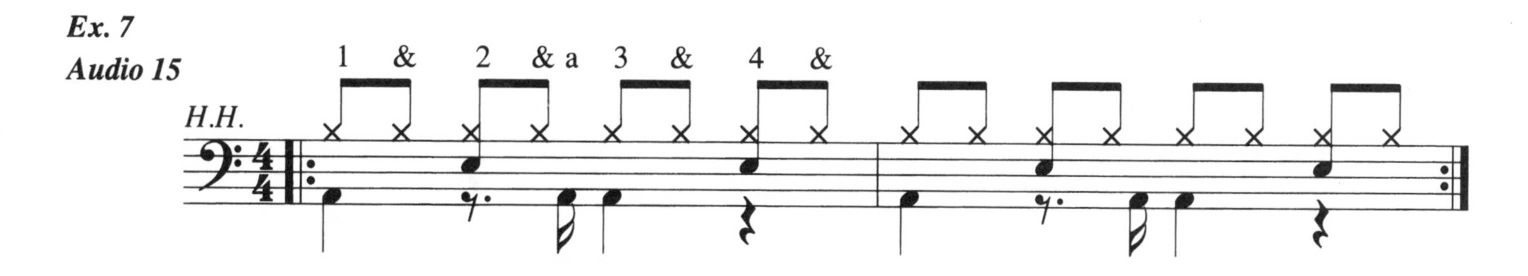

Exercise 8 Audio Track no. 16

In exercise 8 the sixteenth bass drum note falls before beat two and after the & of beat four. Make sure your cymbal rhythm (which is playing eighth notes) remains constant and does not follow the bass drum.

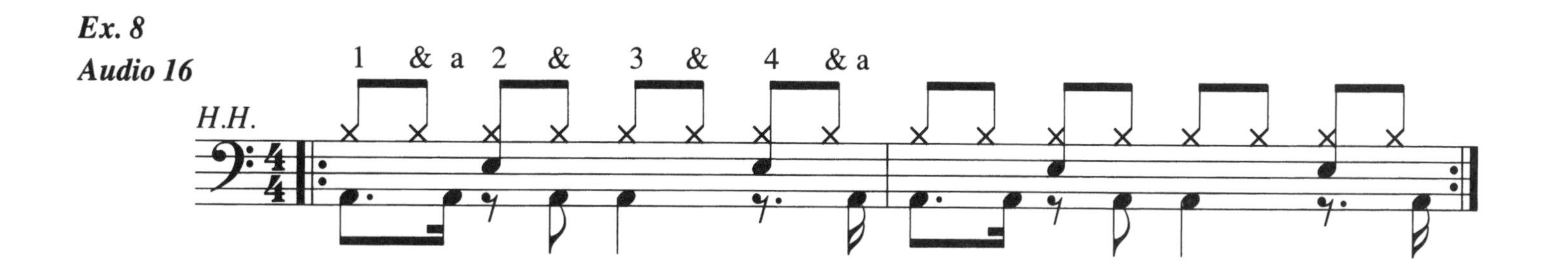

If you have any problems playing these bass drum patterns refer to Part 1 (page 5). Both the height of the drum stool and the position of your foot on the bass pedal can affect your playing. Try to keep as relaxed as possible and don't try to play the exercises too fast at first.
Practise them at different tempos, from 60 bpm to 120 bpm.

HEAVY METAL SIXTEENTH NOTE BASS DRUM PATTERNS (CONTINUED)

Exercise 9 Audio Track nos 17–20

In exercise 9 we have four more bass drum patterns using sixteenth notes.

Ex. 9a
Audio 17

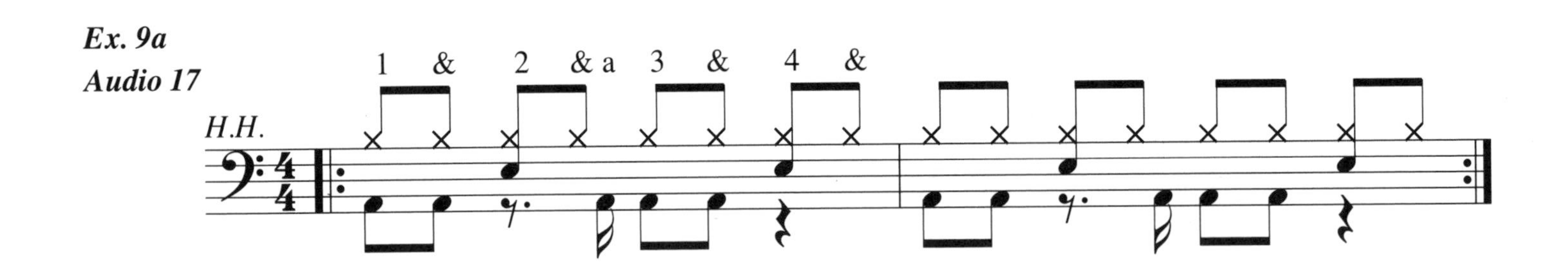

Ex. 9b
Audio 18

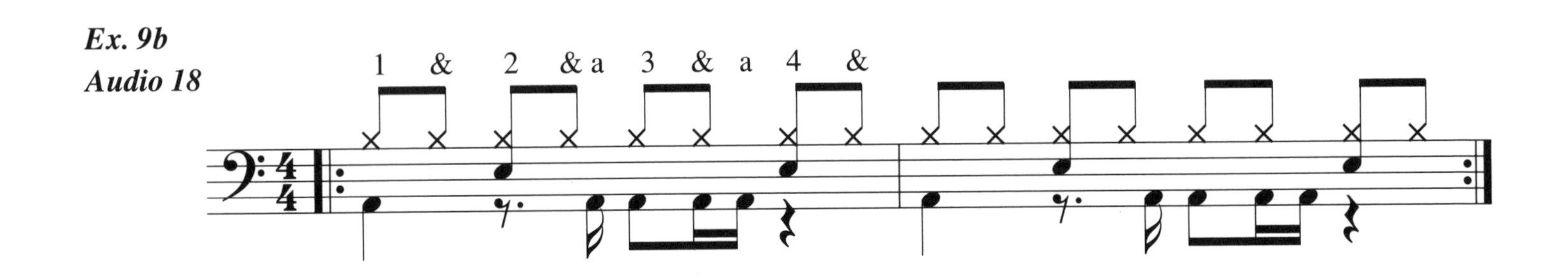

Ex. 9c
Audio 19

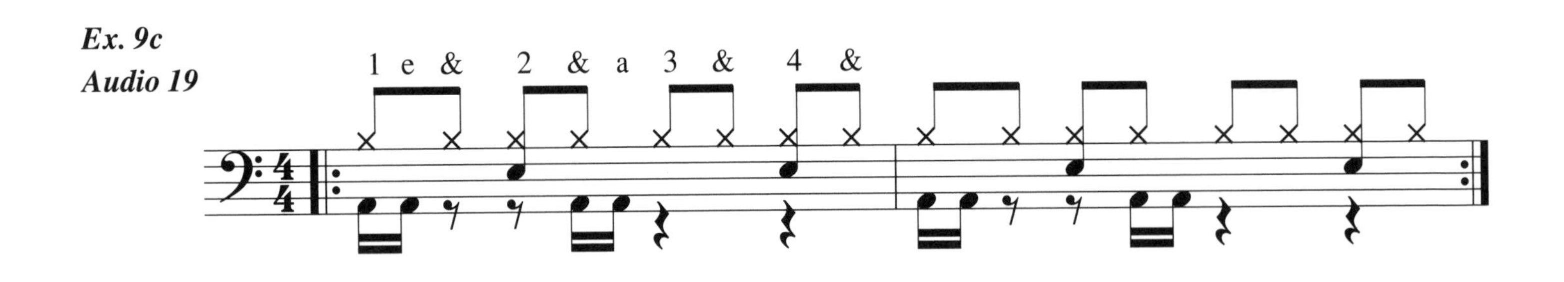

Ex. 9d
Audio 20

For extra practice play from exercise 9a through to exercise 9d without stopping.
For extra practice alternate the cymbal rhythm between the closed hi-hat and ride, play four bars of each.
Practise these rhythms at different tempos, from 60 bpm to 120 bpm.

HEAVY METAL SIXTEENTH NOTE BASS AND SNARE DRUM RHYTHMS

Exercise 10 Audio Track nos 21–24

In exercise 10 we have four syncopated bass and snare drum rhythms using eighth and sixteenth note patterns. Note the half note bass drum rests for beats 3 and 4, as shown in Part 1.

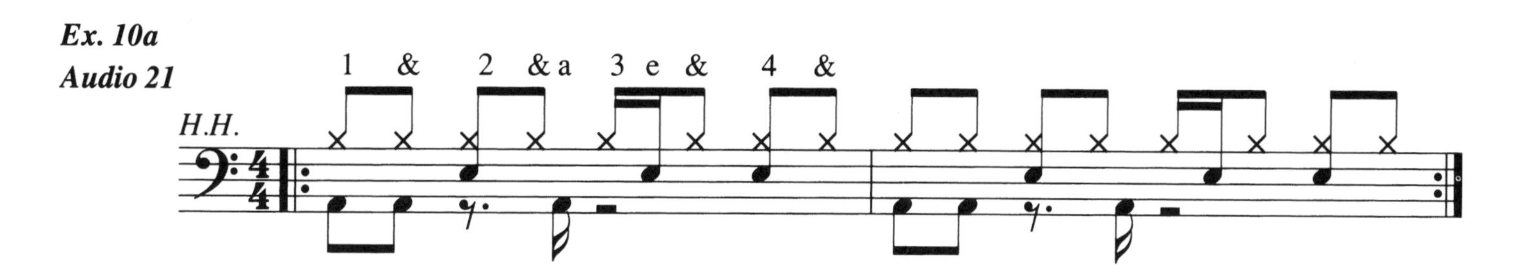

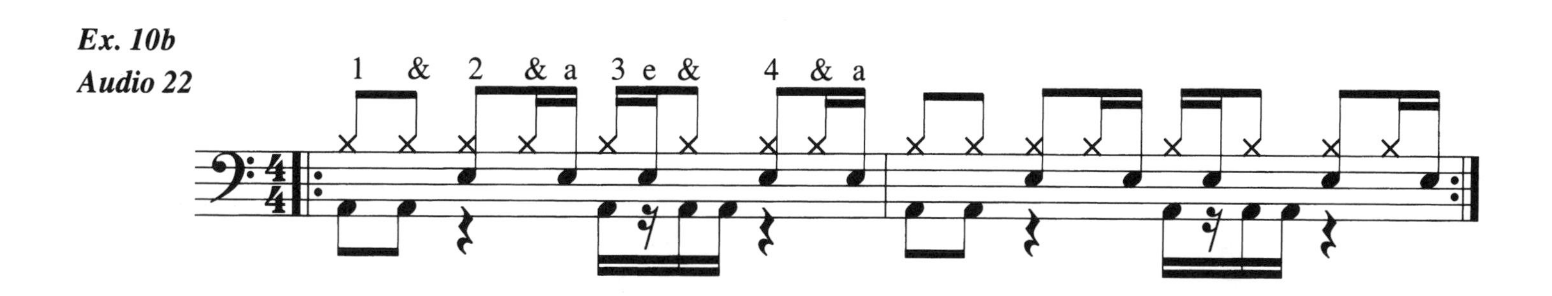

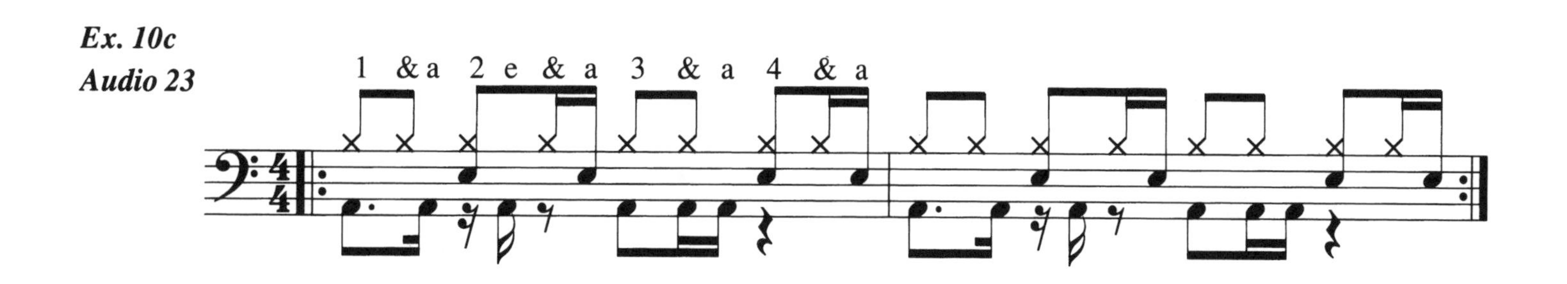

These rhythms are written as one-bar patterns but you can try playing them as two-bar patterns, e.g. Play the first bar of 10a and 10b as one exercise then the first bar of 10c and 10d as another.
For extra practice play all the closed hi-hat patterns on the ride cymbal.
Practise these rhythms at different tempos, from 70 bpm to 120 bpm.

USING SIXTEENTH NOTE BASS AND SNARE DRUM RHYTHMS

Exercise 11 Audio Track nos 25 and 26

Exercise 11 is written in $\frac{4}{4}$ and consists of two parts (A,B,C,D).

In PART A we have a heavy sixteenth note bass drum pattern as practised in exercise 9d for sixteen bars. Note the drum fill in bars eight and sixteen.

In PART B we move onto the ride cymbal and play a two bar-pattern using the rhythms as practised in exercises 10b and 9a. Note these two parts are repeated.

In PART C we play the same rhythm as PART A.

In PART D we play the same rhythm as PART B.

For a good example of the type of rhythms used in this chapter listen to LED ZEPPELIN "When The Levee Breaks", "Immigrant Song", BON JOVI "Keep the Faith", PEARL JAM "Alive", "Why Go" and SOUND GARDEN "Let Me Drown".

Chapter 3

HEAVY METAL SIXTEENTH NOTE HI-HAT PATTERNS

Exercise 12 Audio Track no. 27

So far we have only used eighth note patterns for the cymbal rhythms. In exercise 12 we have a pattern of sixteenth notes on the hi-hat played with hand to hand sticking (RLRL etc.). On beats 2 and 4 the right hand drops down to play the snare while the left hand remains on the hi-hat. The bass drum falls on beats 1 and 3. Keep the hi-hat closed quite tight at all times to produce a clean sound.

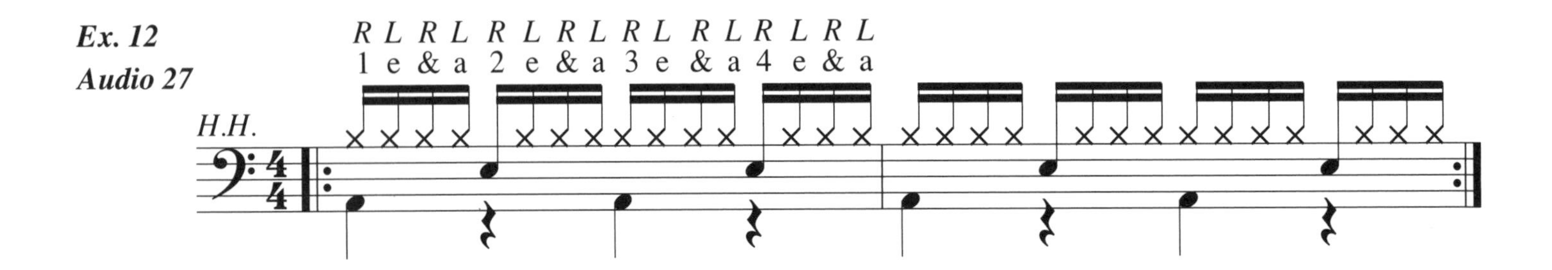

Exercise 13 Audio Track no. 28

In exercise 13 we have a different bass drum pattern. It plays on beats 1, 2, 3, 4.

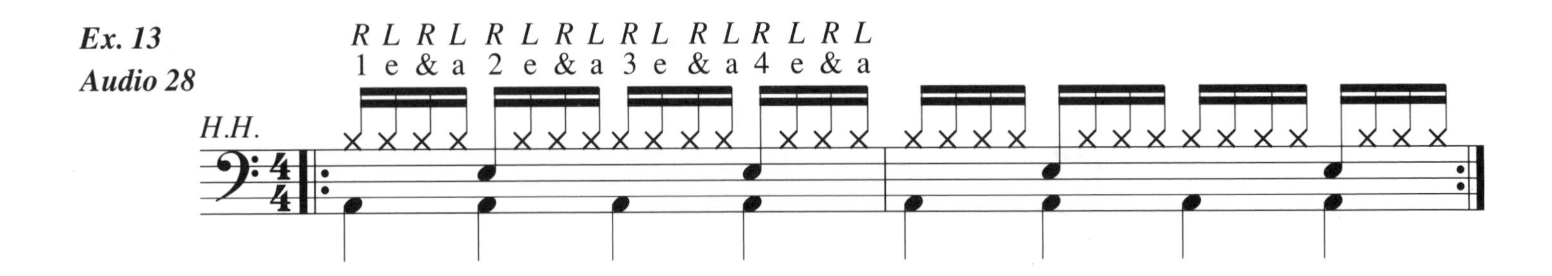

When playing these rhythms it is important to get the right balance in sound between the hi-hat, bass and snare drum. The hi-hat should be played quite lightly, with the snare and bass drum at stronger, equal volumes to produce a good solid feel.
Practise these rhythms at different tempos, from 80 bpm to 130 bpm.

HEAVY METAL SIXTEENTH NOTE HI-HAT RHYTHMS WITH BASS DRUM VARIATIONS

Exercise 14 Audio Track nos 29–32

In exercise 14 we have four bass drum variations. Make sure every bass drum beat is played exactly in time with the sixteenth note hi-hat rhythm.

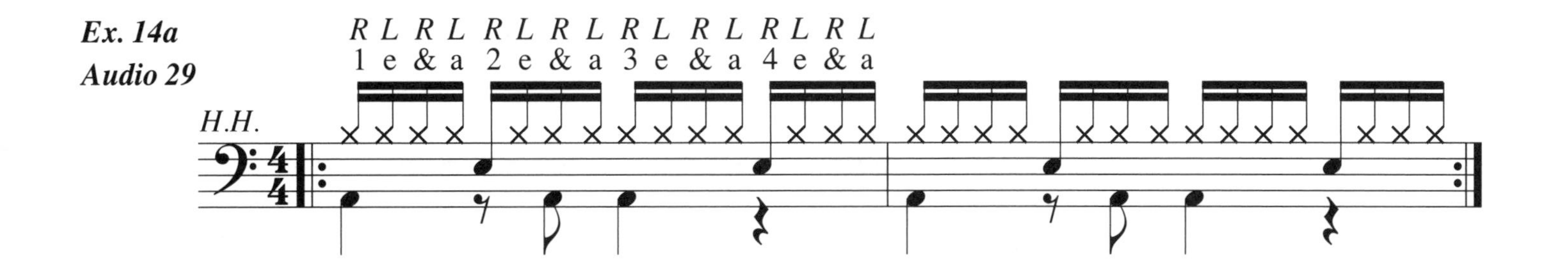

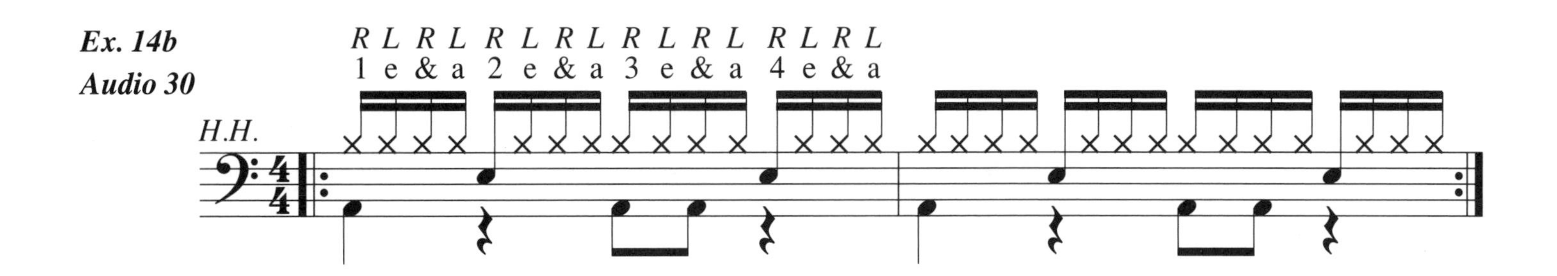

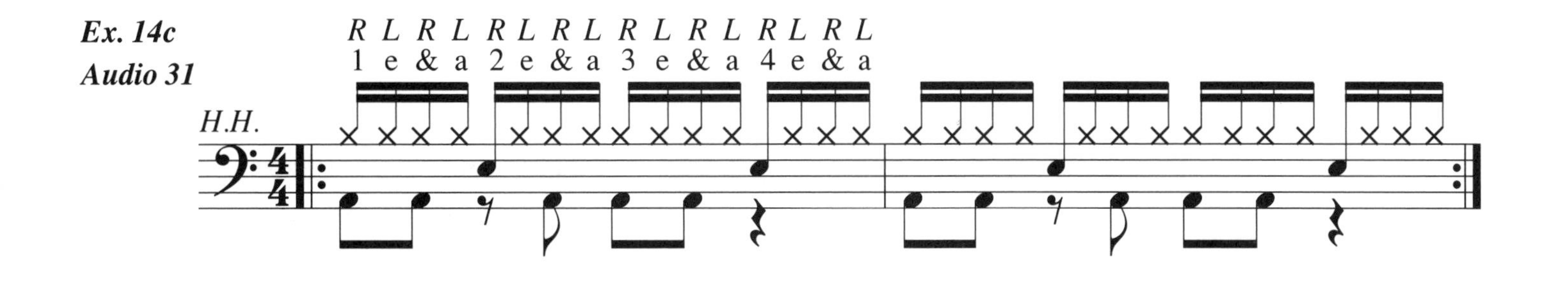

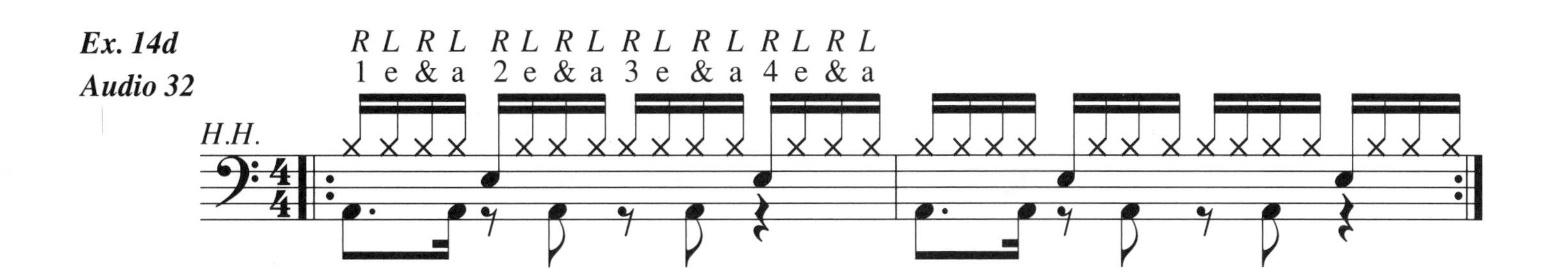

Practise these rhythms at different tempos, from 80 bpm to 130 bpm.

HEAVY METAL SIXTEENTH NOTE HI-HAT RHYTHMS WITH SNARE DRUM VARIATIONS

Exercise 15 Audio Track nos 33–36

In exercise 15 we have four sixteenth note hi-hat rhythms with snare drum variations. The sticking is played hand to hand (RLRL etc.) with the bass drum playing a steady quarter note pattern throughout.
Note in these exercises the snare is played with the right and left hands.

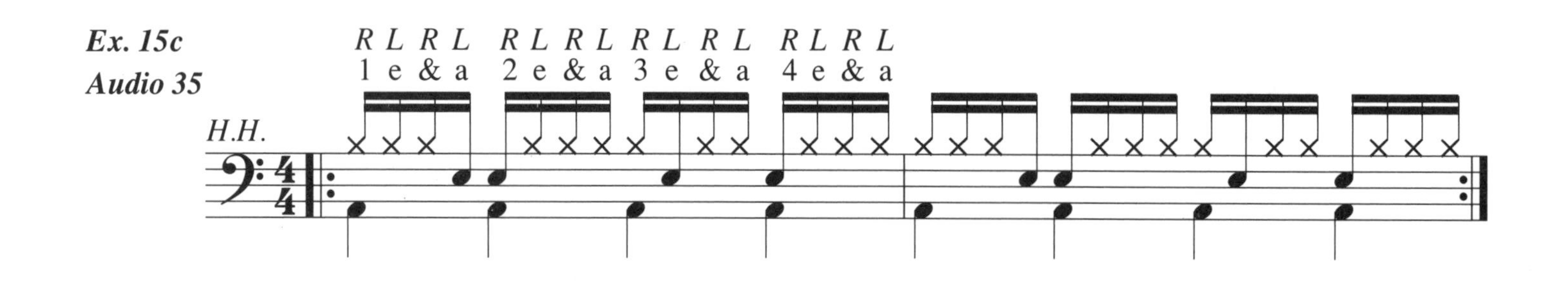

Practise these rhythms at different tempos, from 80 bpm to 130 bpm.

USING SIXTEENTH NOTE HI-HAT PATTERNS

Exercise 16 Audio Track nos 37 and 38

Exercise 16 is written in $\frac{4}{4}$ and consists of four eight-bar sections (A,B,C,D).

In PART A we have a sixteenth note hi-hat pattern as practised in exercise 12.

In PART B we move to a sixteenth note pattern with a busier bass drum rhythm, as practised in exercise 14d.

In PART C we play the same rhythm as in section A.

In PART D we have a rhythm as practised in exercise 14c.

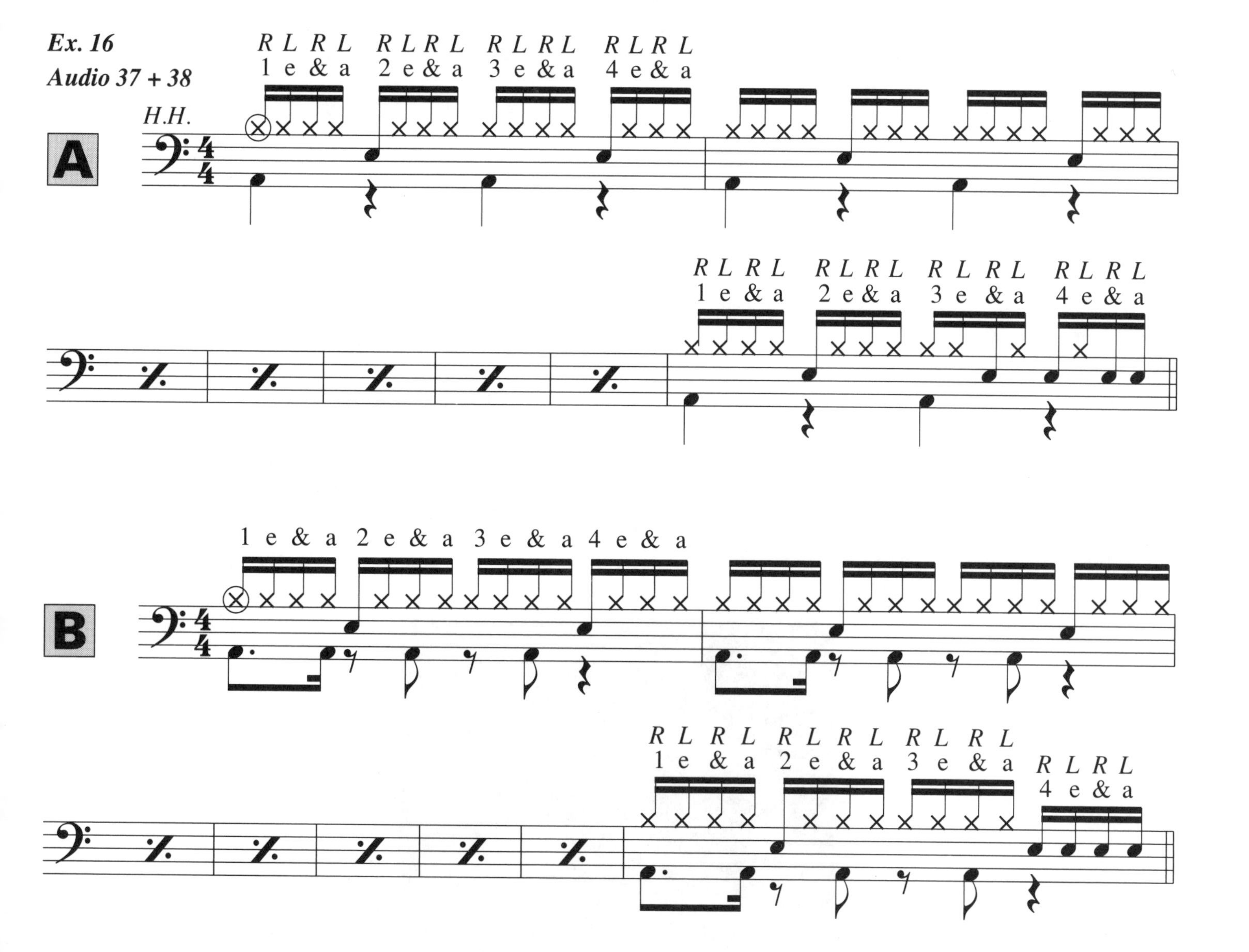

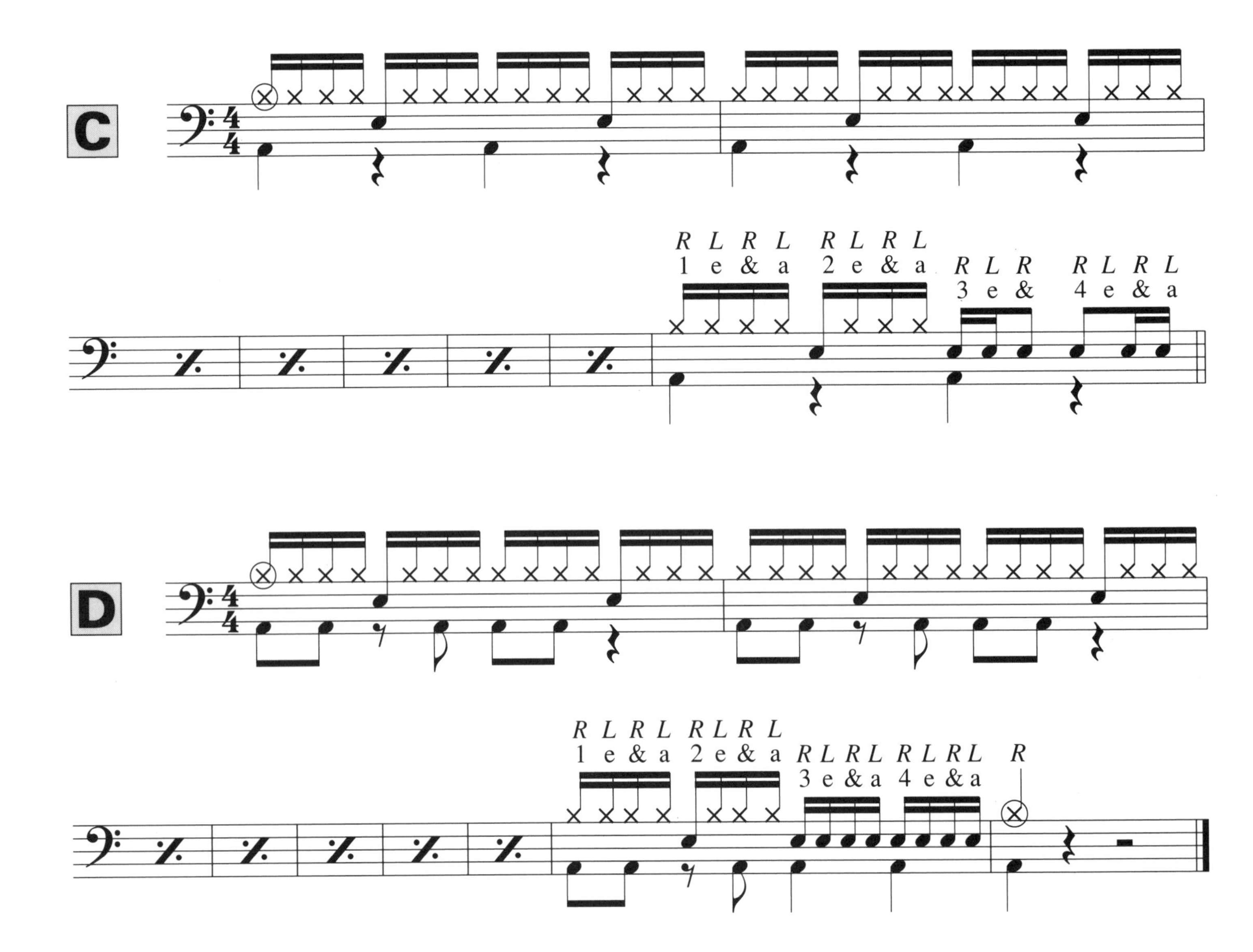

For a good example of the type of rhythms used in exercises 12–15 listen to BIG COUNTRY “Rain Dance”, “Chance”, DEEP PURPLE “Smoke on the Water” and SIMPLE MINDS “All The Things She Said”.

Mark Brezicki, Big Country (Redferns)

SIXTEENTH NOTE HI-HAT PATTERNS (FOR SLOW TEMPOS)

Exercise 17 Audio Track no. 39

When playing songs that are in a very slow tempo, eighth note cymbal patterns might feel uncomfortably slow to play, so a sixteenth note cymbal pattern is often used.
In exercise 17 the hi-hat pattern (playing sixteenth notes) is played with your right hand only. The snare is played with your left hand.

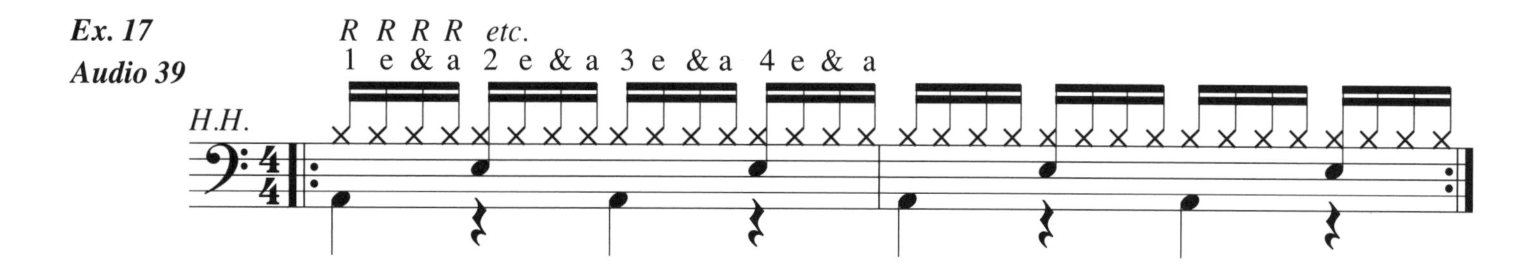

Exercise 18 Audio Track no. 40

In exercise 18 we have a bass drum variation. Note in both these exercises the hi-hat and snare play simultaneously on beats 2 and 4.

Practise these rhythms at different tempos, from 40 bpm to 70 bpm.

SIXTEENTH NOTES HI-HAT PATTERNS (FOR SLOW TEMPOS) (CONTINUED)

Exercise 19 Audio Track nos 41–44

In exercise 19 we have four more bass drum variations using sixteenth note hi-hat patterns for slow tempos.

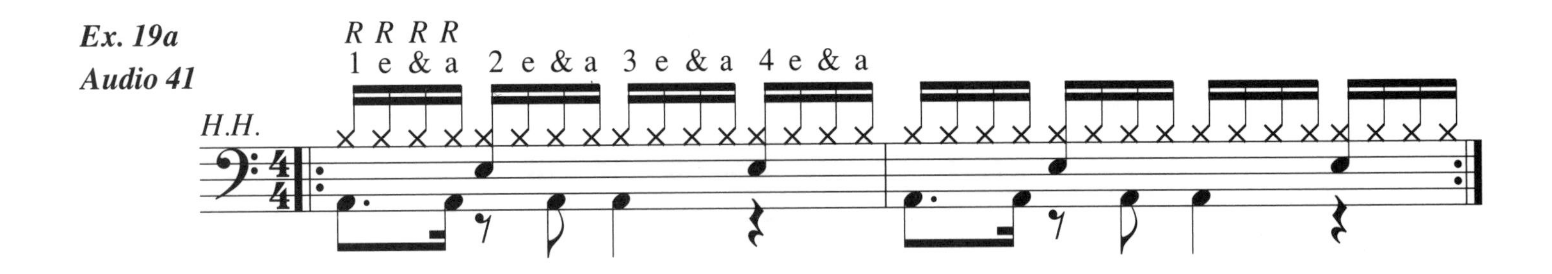

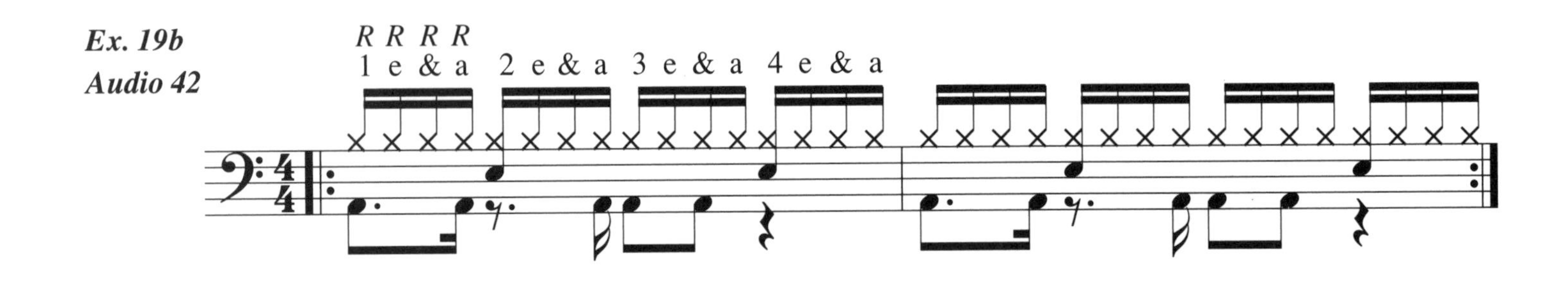

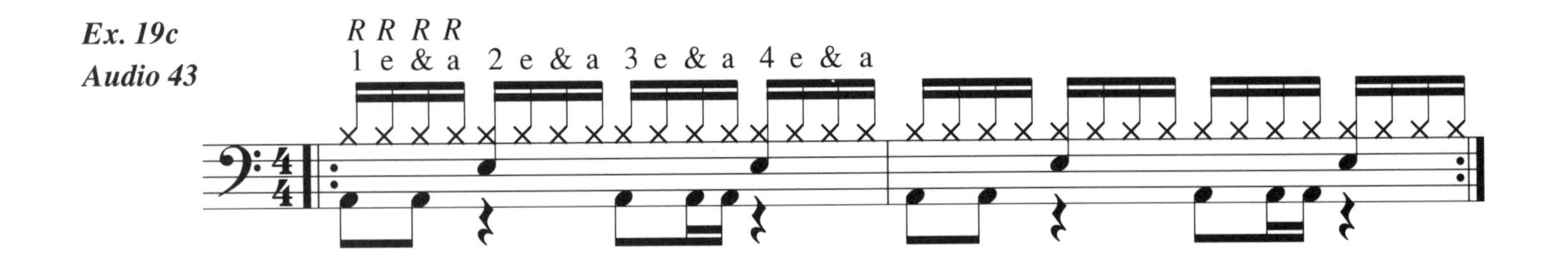

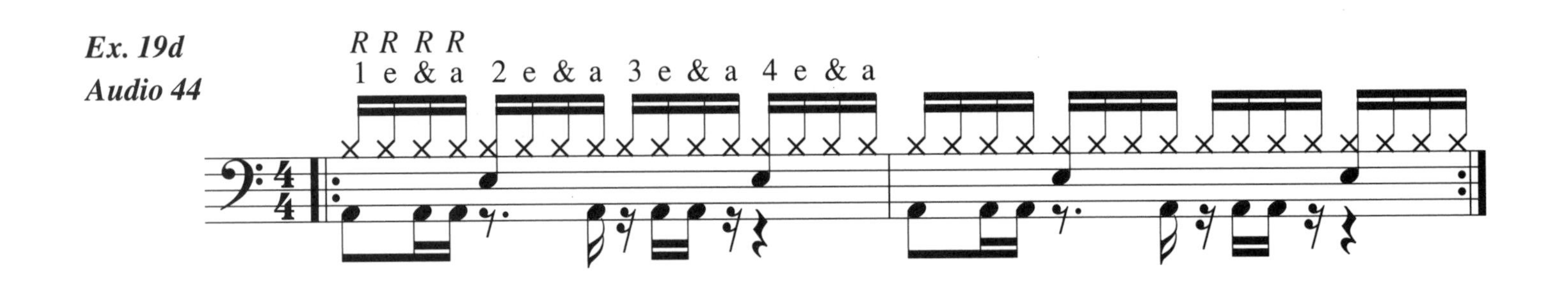

For extra practice play from exercise 19a through to exercise 19d without stopping.
Practise these rhythms at different tempos, from 40 bpm to 70 bpm.

USING SIXTEENTH NOTE HI-HAT PATTERNS (FOR SLOW TEMPOS)

Exercise 20 Audio Track nos 45 and 46

Exercise 20 is written in $\frac{4}{4}$ and it consists of four parts (A, B, C, D).

In PART A we have a slow and heavy rhythm as used in exercise 19a.

In PART B we move to a sixteenth note ride cymbal rhythm with a busier bass drum pattern as practised in exercise 19d. Note the three-beat rest in bar sixteen.

In PART C we play the same rhythm as in part A.

In PART D we move onto the ride cymbal and play the same rhythm as in part B for the last eight bars.

For a good example of the type of rhythms used in exercises 17–19 listen to PINK FLOYD "What Do You Want From Me", and RED HOT CHILLI PEPPERS "Blood Sugar Sex Magik".

Chapter 4

SIXTEENTH NOTE SNARE DRUM PATTERNS

Exercise 21 Audio Track no. 47

In exercise 21 we have a six-bar snare drum exercise (which is repeated) using sixteenth notes and rests played hand to hand (RLRL etc.). The bass drum plays a quarter note pattern throughout. Try to play all the snare beats close to the centre of the drum with equal volume and say the count aloud as you play.

Ex. 21
Audio 47

For extra practice play all the snare beats starting with the left hand (LRLR etc.).
Practise this exercise at different tempos, from 50 bpm to 120 bpm.

HEAVY METAL SIXTEENTH AND EIGHTH NOTE SNARE DRUM FILLS

Exercise 22 Audio Track no. 48

In exercise 22 we have a bar of rhythm followed by a one-bar drum fill. The bass drum and hi-hat play the same pattern throughout both bars.

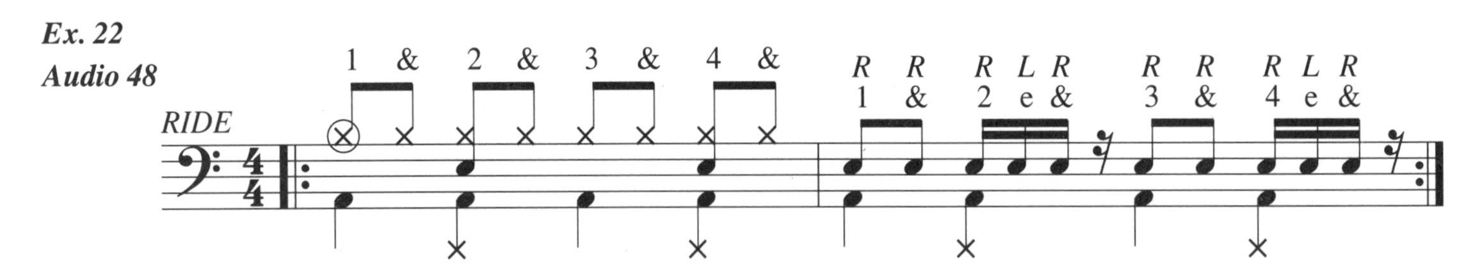

Exercise 23 Audio Track no. 49

In exercise 23 we have a variation on the one-bar drum fill.

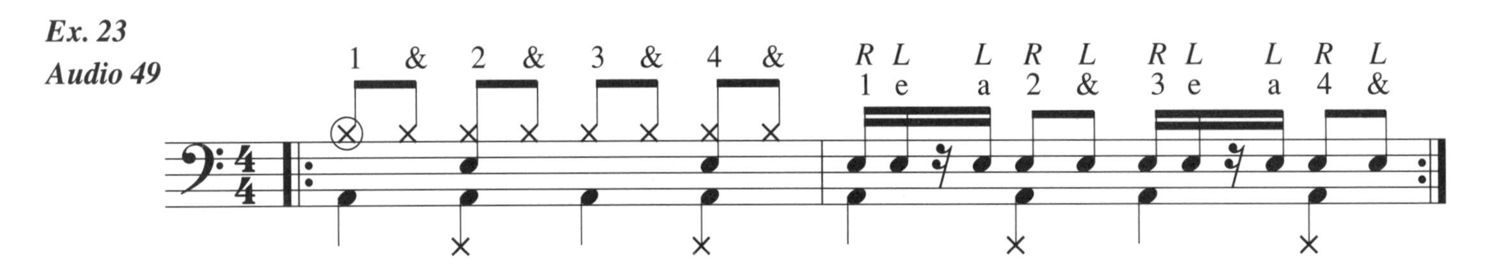

For extra practice substitute the one-bar rhythm patterns with any of the previous rhythms in chapter one or two.
Practise these exercises at different tempos, from 80 bpm to 130 bpm.

Chad Smith, Red Hot Chili Peppers (Redferns)

HEAVY METAL SIXTEENTH AND EIGHTH NOTE SNARE DRUM FILLS (CONTINUED)

Exercise 24 Audio Track no. 50

In exercises 24 and 25 we have two more variations on the one-bar drum fill.

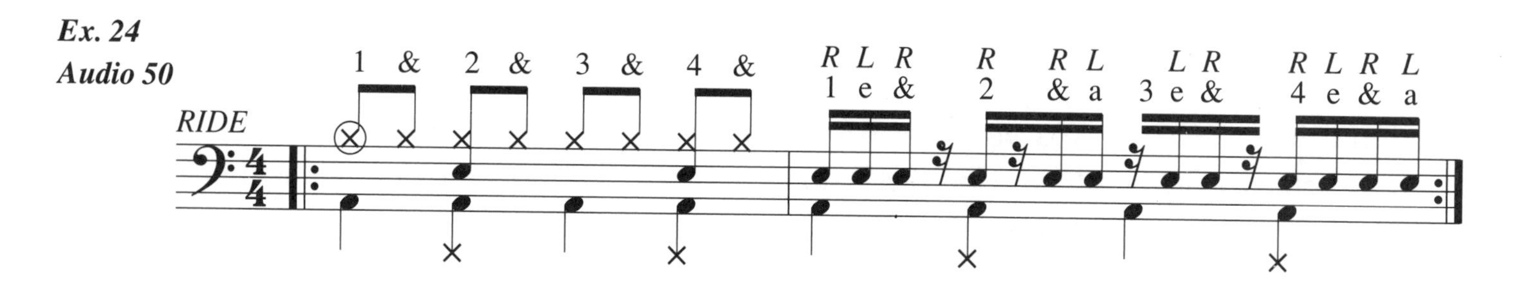

Exercise 25 Audio Track no. 51

For extra practice alternate the cymbal rhythm between the ride and closed hi-hat.
For extra practice play three or seven bars of rhythm before the one-bar drum fill.
Practise these exercises at different tempos, from 80 bpm to 130 bpm.

HEAVY METAL SIXTEENTH NOTE TRIPLET DRUM FILLS FOR SLOW TEMPOS

Exercise 26 Audio Track no. 52

When playing songs at very slow tempos, straight sixteenth or eighth note fills (as practised in the previous exercises) might feel uncomfortably slow to play, so you will find sixteenth note triplet fills more appropriate.

In exercise 26 we have a sixteenth note triplet fill played on the snare in the second bar on beat four. When playing the fill, accent* the first beat of each triplet (as shown), this will help you get the feel of the triplet and keep it in time.

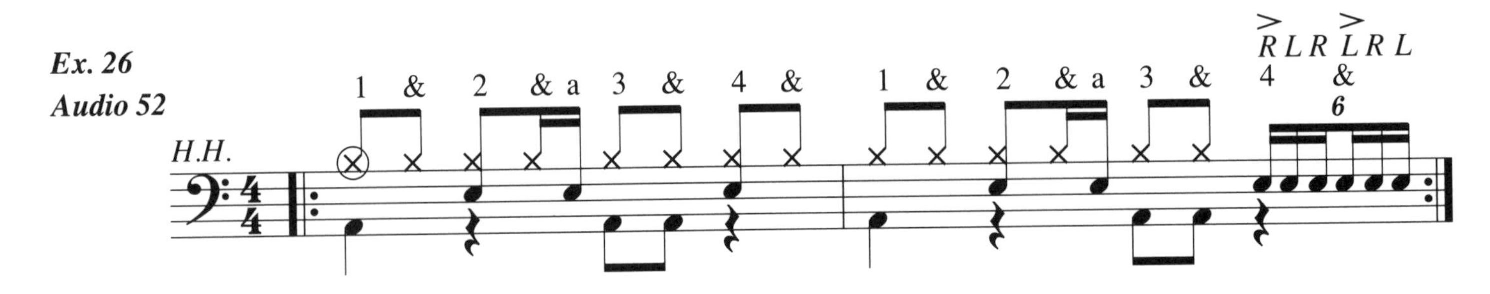

Exercise 27 Audio Track no. 53

In exercise 27 the triplet fill starts on beat three of the second bar. Note the toms are played on beats three and four.

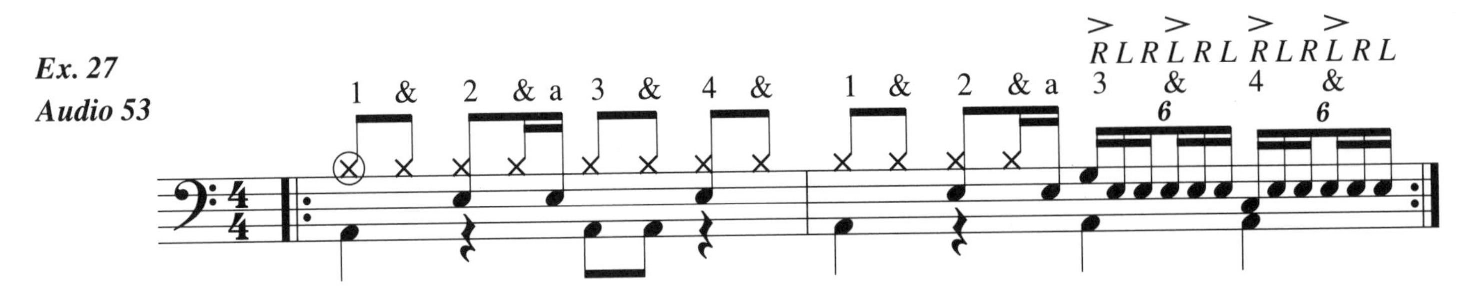

For extra practice play three or seven bars of rhythm before playing the bar with the drum fill. Practise these exercises at different tempos, from 55 bpm to 95 bpm.

---

*When the accent sign > is placed above a note it indicates that the note is to be played louder than the notes without accents.

USING SIXTEENTH AND EIGHTH NOTE SNARE DRUM FILLS

Exercise 28 Audio Track nos 54 and 55

Exercise 28 is written in $\frac{4}{4}$ and consists of two parts (A,B) which are repeated.

In PART A we have a two-bar rhythm with the hi-hat playing a quarter note pattern (shown in Book 1.) The drum fill in bar eight is the same as bar two of exercise 24.
Note the drum fill in bar one starts on beat three. On the audio track you will hear a four-beat count at the start plus two beats before the fill.

In PART B we move onto the ride cymbal and play six bars of rhythm with a two-bar drum fill. Note the rhythm of the two-bar fill is the same as bar two of exercise 25.

Matt Cameron, Soundgarden (Redferns)

Ex. 28
Audio 54 + 55
H.H.
A
R L L R L
1 2 3 e a 4 &
1 2 3 & 4 1 2 3 & 4 &
2
R L R R R L L R R L R L
1 e & 2 & a 3 e & 4 e & a
B
RIDE
1 & 2 & a 3 & 4 &
R L L R R L L R L L
1 e a 2 & a 3 e & 4 &

Chapter 5

DRUM RUDIMENTS

THE PARADIDDLE

Exercise 29 Audio Track no. 56

This rudiment is called a paradiddle because of the sticking used to play it: RLRRLRLL. This is a two-bar exercise, bar A playing eighth notes and bar B playing sixteenth notes. Make sure every beat is even in tempo and volume.

Exercise 30 Audio Track no. 57

In exercise 30 we have added the bass drum (playing quarter notes) and hi-hat (falling on beats 2 and 4) to the paradiddle pattern played on the snare.

For extra practice start both the above exercises with your left hand e.g. LRLLRLRR. Practise these exercises at different tempos, from 50 bpm to 140 bpm.

PARADIDDLES AROUND THE KIT

Exercise 31 Audio Track no. 58

In exercise 31 we have a bar of rhythm followed by a one-bar, sixteenth note drum fill played with paradiddle sticking. Note the toms play on beats 1,2,3,4.

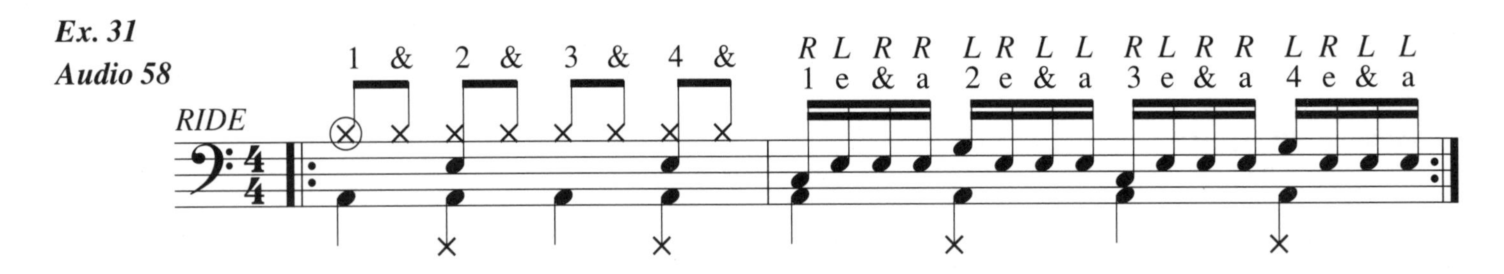

Exercise 32 Audio Track no. 59

In exercise 32 we have a variation on the paradiddle drum fill.

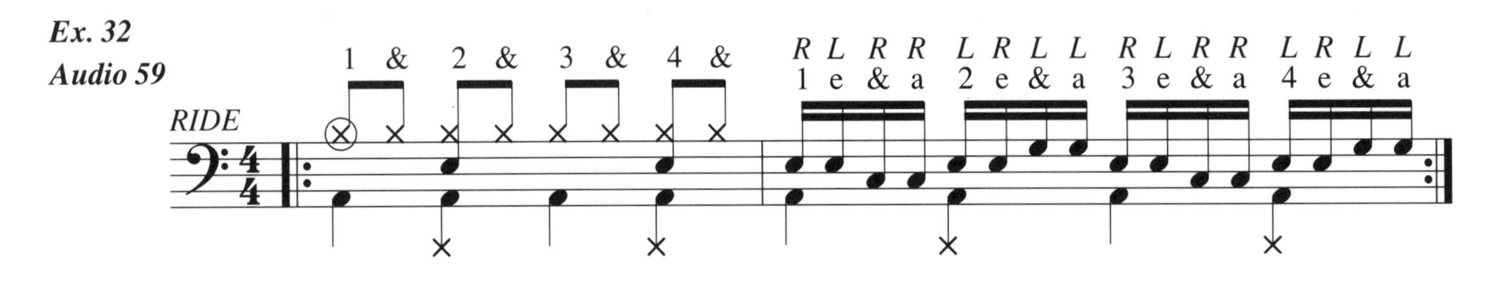

Exercise 33 Audio Track no. 60

In exercise 33 we have another variation on the sixteenth note paradiddle fill.
This time the fill starts on beat three.

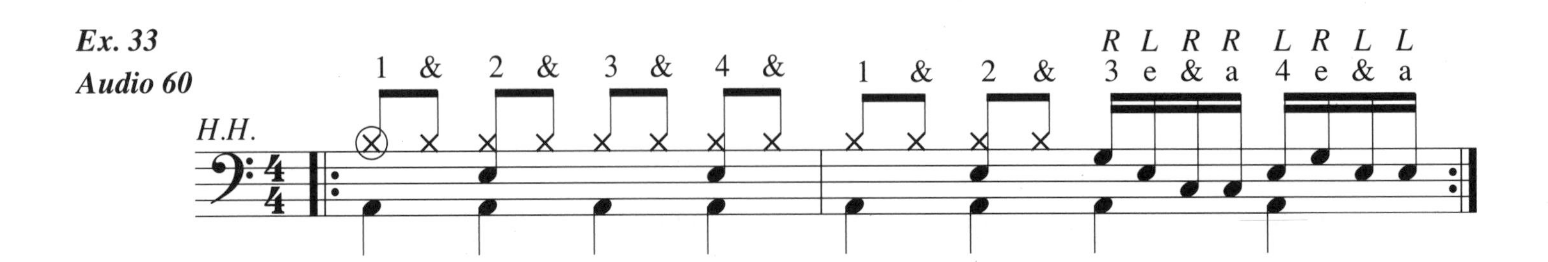

Practise these rhythms at different tempos, from 60 bpm to 120 bpm.

Exercise 34 Audio Track no. 61

In exercise 34 we have a paradiddle played between the right foot (on the bass drum) and the left hand (on the snare). Make sure the closed hi-hat (played with your right hand) plays a constant eighth note pattern and does not follow the bass drum pattern.

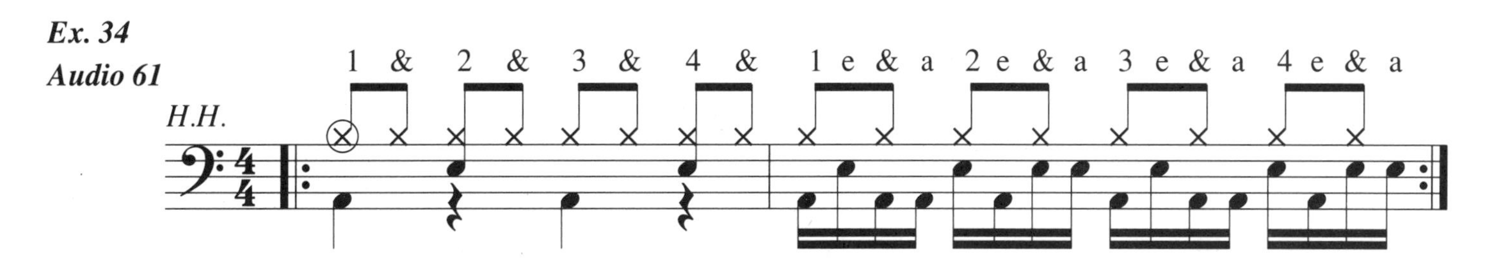

For extra practice play exercises 31–34 with three bars of rhythm before the paradiddle fills.
For extra practice alternate the cymbal rhythm between the closed hi-hat and the ride.
Practise these exercises at different tempos, from 60 bpm to 120 bpm.
Note in exercise 34 the snare drum has been written with the tail part of the notes pointing down, this is just to make it easier to read. Drum notes can be written with the tail pointing up or down.

John Bonham, Led Zeppelin

THE FLAM

Exercise 35 Audio Track no. 62

The flam consists of a main (accented) note preceded by a grace note (shown as a smaller note). The grace note should be played very lightly and as close to the main note as possible. However, at the beginning keep the two notes apart, gradually bringing them closer together as you become more proficient.
When played correctly the flam should sound like one fat heavy note.

In exercise 35 note the flam is played with alternating hands.

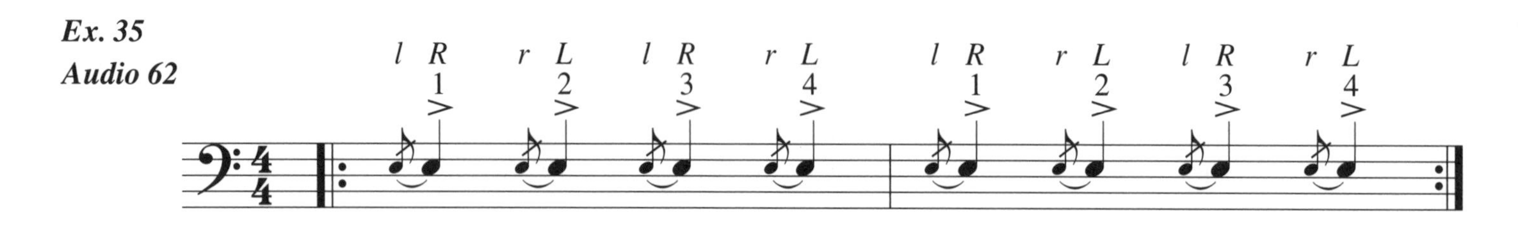

Exercise 36 Audio no. 63

In exercise 36 we have a flam followed by an eighth note bass drum pattern.

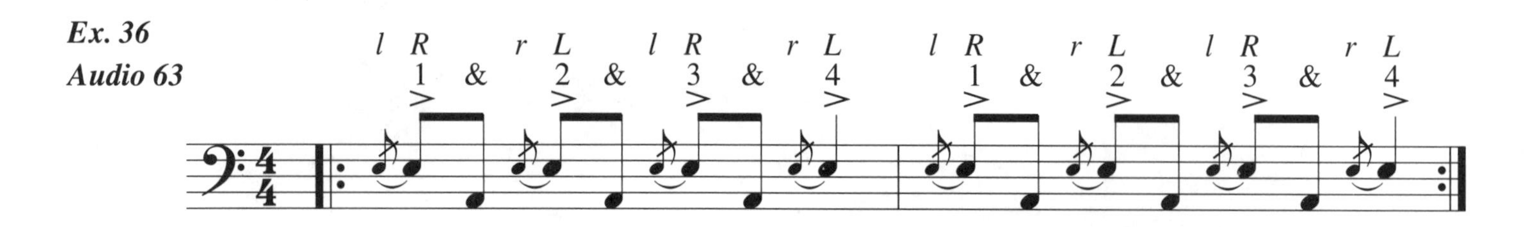

For extra practice play the flams starting with your right hand e.g. rL, lR etc.
Practise these exercises at different tempos, from 50 bpm to 120 bpm.

Exercise 37 Audio Track no. 64

In exercise 37 we have a drum fill played between the snare and bass drum incorporating the flam.

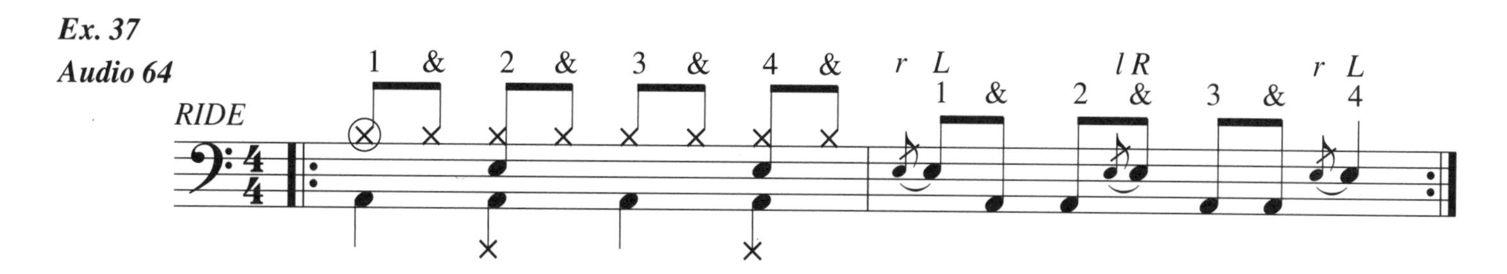

Exercise 38 Audio Track no. 65

In exercise 38 we have another fill using the flam as part of a sixteenth and eighth note pattern between the snare and bass drum.

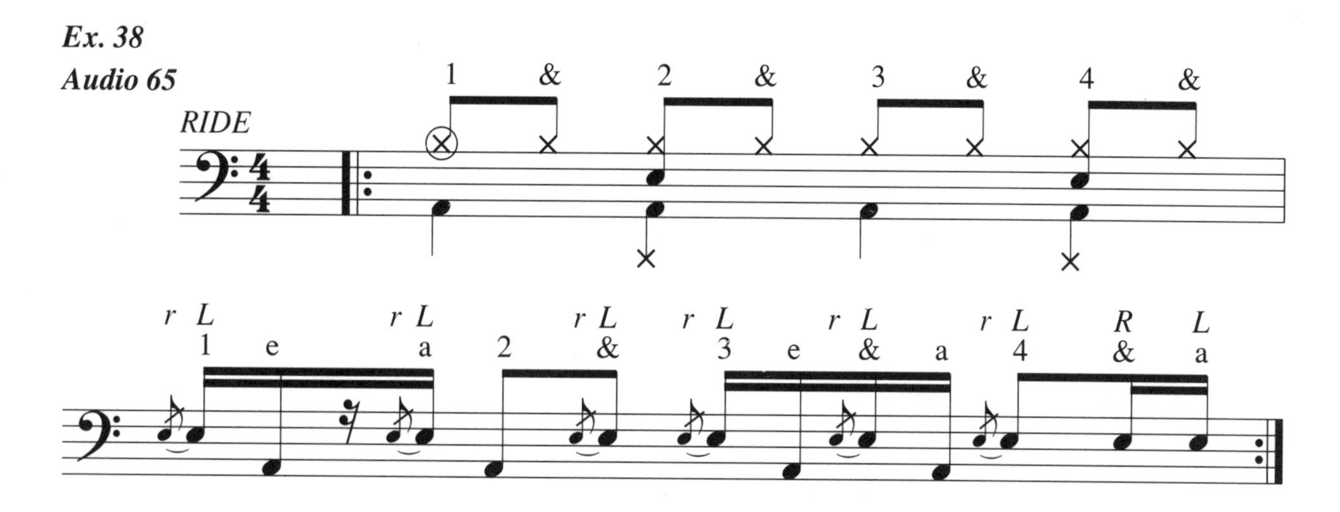

For extra practice play three or seven bars of rhythm before the fill.
Practise these exercises at different tempos, from 60 bpm to 120 bpm.

THE FOUR STROKE RUFF

Exercise 39 Audio Track no. 66

The four stroke ruff consists of four beats played hand to hand (RLRL) with an accent on the fourth note.
Start your practise playing the ruff slowly and evenly, gradually increasing the tempo as you become more proficient.

Ex. 39
Audio 66

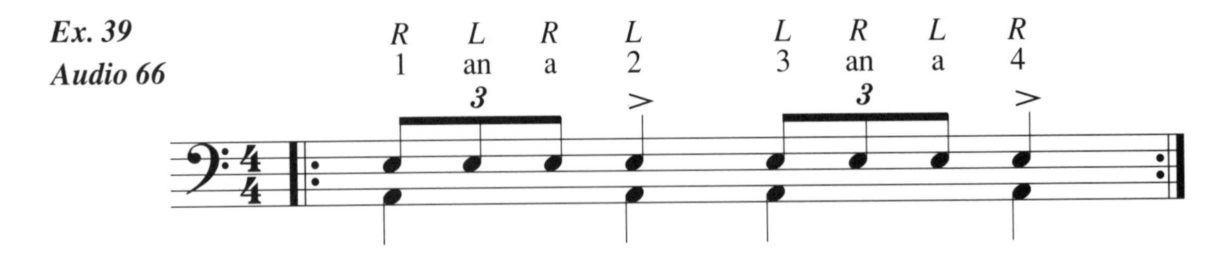

Exercise 40 Audio Track no. 67

In exercise 40 we have the four stroke ruff playing sixteenth note triplets.

Ex. 40
Audio 67

Exercise 41 Audio Track no. 68

In exercise 41 the four stroke ruff starts on the & of beat one.

Ex. 41
Audio 68

Practise these exercises at different tempos, from 50 bpm to 100 bpm.

THE FOUR STROKE RUFF AROUND THE KIT

Exercise 42 Audio Track no. 69

In exercise 42 we have the four stroke ruff used as a one-bar fill played around the kit.

Exercise 43 Audio Track no. 70

In exercise 43 the four stroke ruff starts on the & and is played between the snare and toms with every fourth note played on the bass drum.

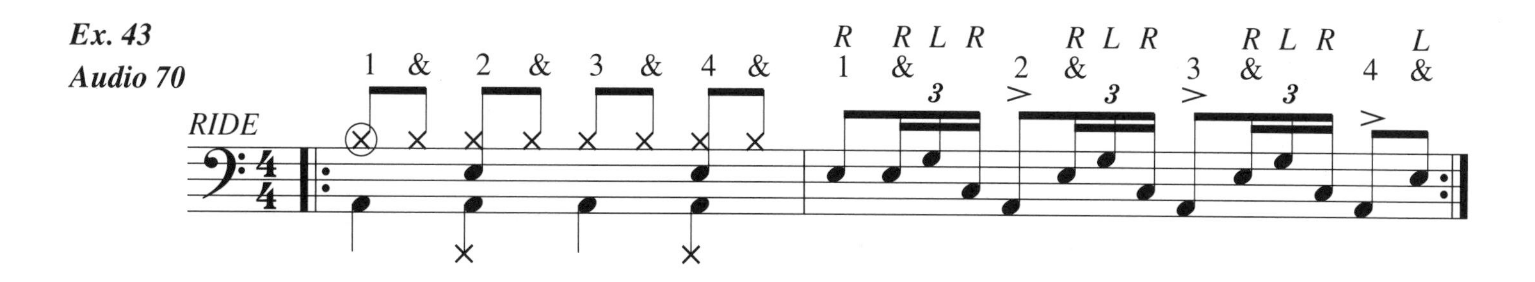

For extra practice play three or seven bars of rhythm before the one-bar fill.
For extra practice alternate the cymbal rhythm between the ride and the closed hi-hat.
Practise these exercises at different tempos, from 50 bpm to 100 bpm.

DRUM INTROS

Exercise 44 Audio Track no. 71

When playing with a band the drummer will often start a song by counting a bar of time (e.g. 1,2,3,4) at the required tempo or play a drum fill into the first beat of the song. In exercise 44 we have a simple but effective four beat drum fill leading into the rhythm bar.

Ex. 44
Audio 71

Exercise 45 Audio Track no. 72

In exercise 45 we have another four-beat drum intro. Note the use of the flams which are played on the snare drum.

Ex. 45
Audio 72

For extra practice try playing different rhythms after each of the drum fills.
Practise these exercises at different tempos, from 70 bpm to 120 bpm.

DRUM INTROS (CONTINUED)

Exercise 46 Audio Track no. 73

In exercise 46 we have a two-beat drum intro. Note the sticking is similar to the first half of a single paradiddle.

Ex. 46
Audio 73

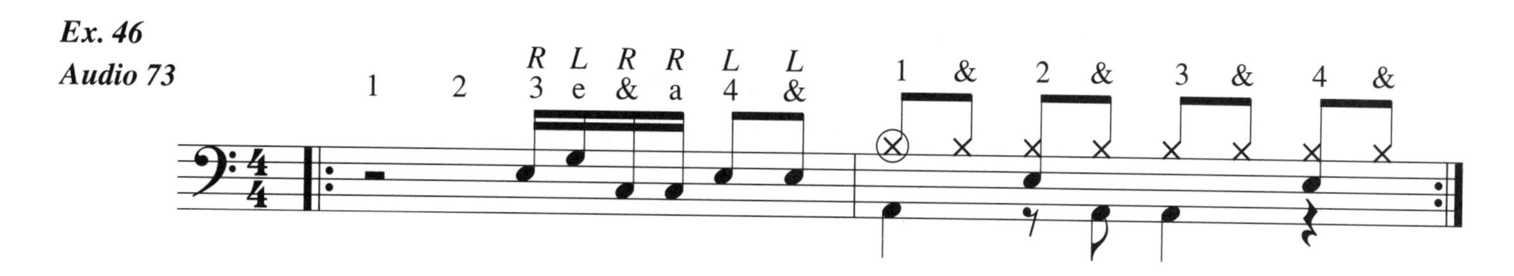

Exercise 47 Audio Track no. 74

In exercise 47 we have another two-beat drum intro incorporating a flam and a four stroke ruff played around the kit.

Ex. 47
Audio 74

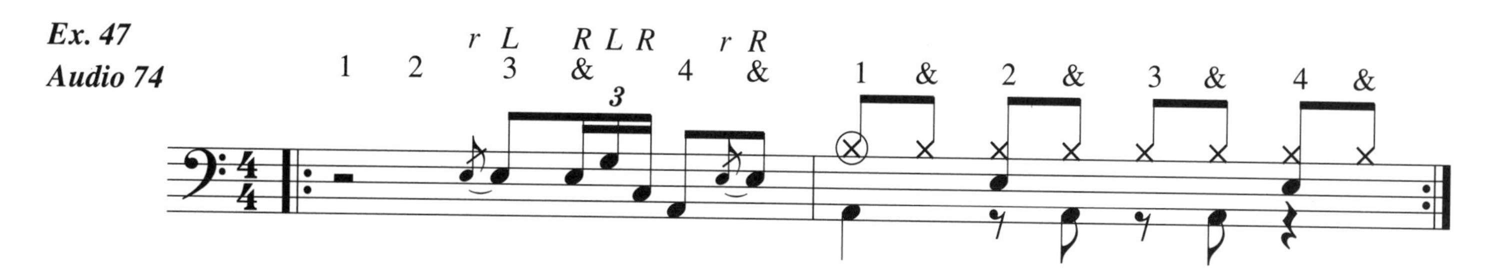

For extra practice try playing different rhythms after each of the drum fills.
Practise these exercises at different tempos, from 70 bpm to 120 bpm.

For some good examples of drum intros listen to PEARL JAM “Glorified”, “Why Go”, LED ZEPPELIN “When The Levee Breaks”, BIG COUNTRY “In A Big Country” and SIMPLE MINDS “Oh Jungleland”.

Chapter 6

OPEN HI-HAT RHYTHMS

Exercise 48 Audio Track no. 75

When the letter O is placed above a hi-hat note it means play that beat with the hi-hat cymbals open. When a + sign is placed above a hi-hat note you close the hi-hat cymbals together. When playing an open hi-hat beat let the cymbals part only an inch or two, do not take your foot completely off the pedal. Keep the cymbals closed quite tightly on all the other beats. In exercise 48 the hi-hat opens on the & of beat three and closes on beat four (simultaneously with the bass drum).

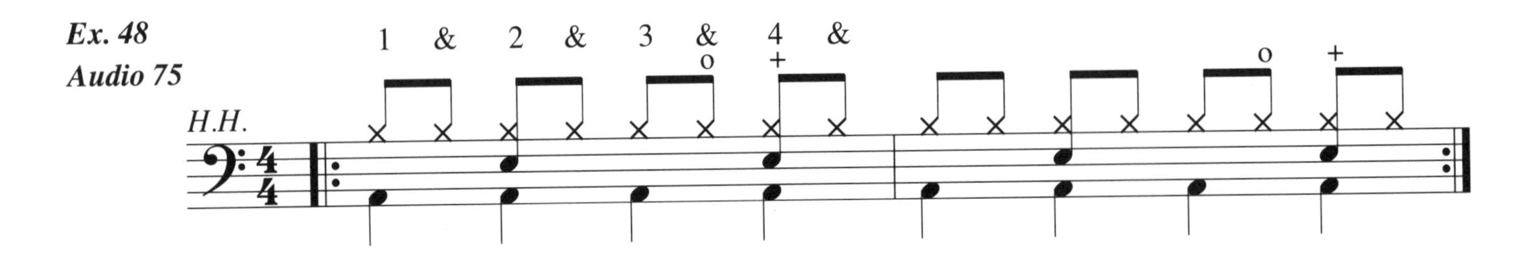

Exercise 49 Audio Track no. 76

In exercise 49 the hi-hat opens on the & of beat one and closes on beat two.

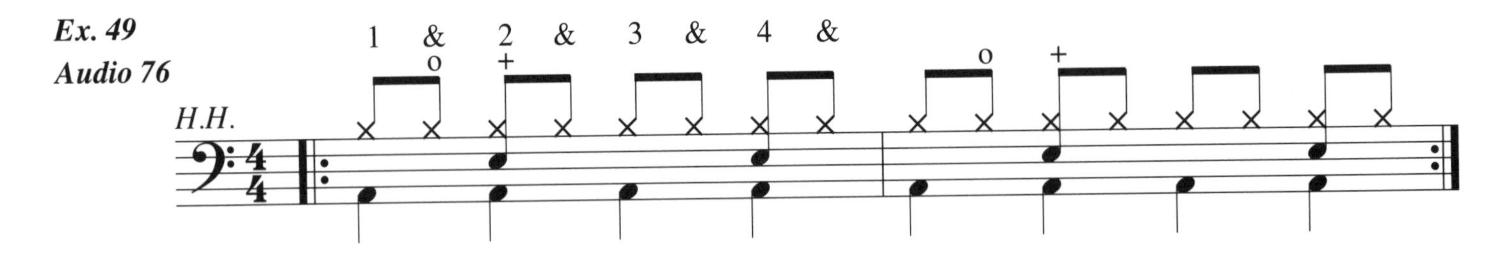

Practise these rhythms at different tempos, from 70 bpm to 120 bpm.

OPEN HI-HAT RHYTHMS (CONTINUED)

Exercise 50 Audio Track nos 77–80

In exercise 50 we have four more open hi-hat patterns. Note in exercises 50c and 50d the hi-hat opens on two beats in each bar.

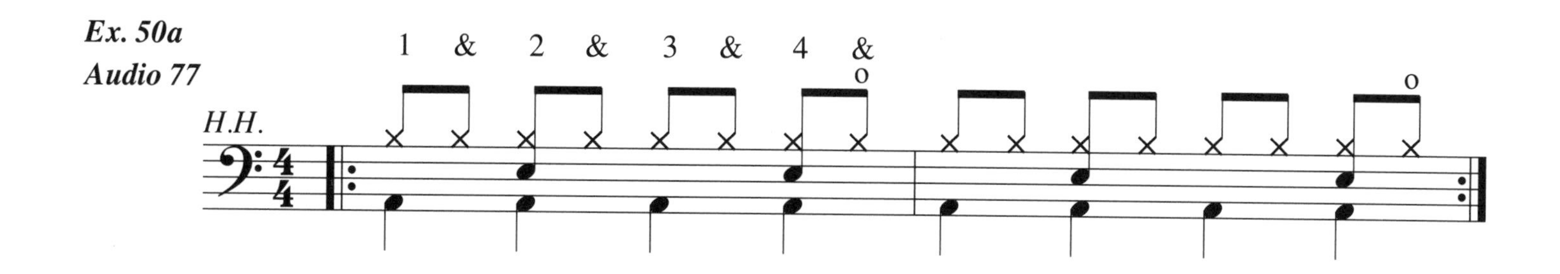

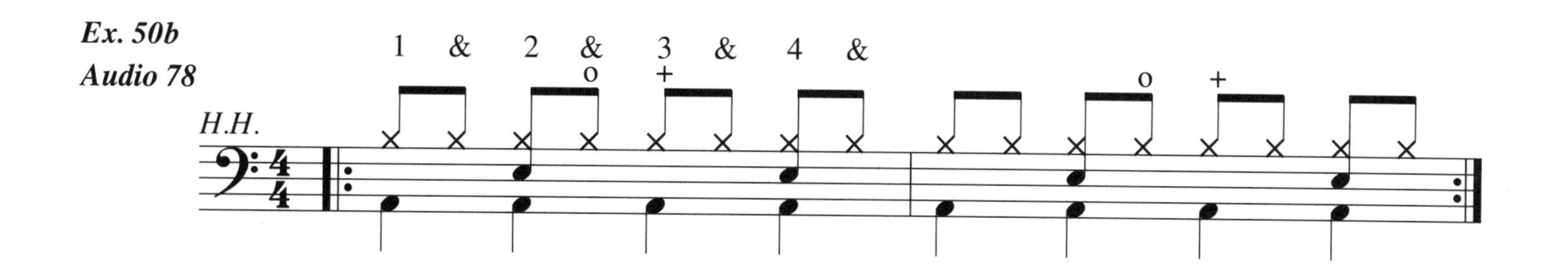

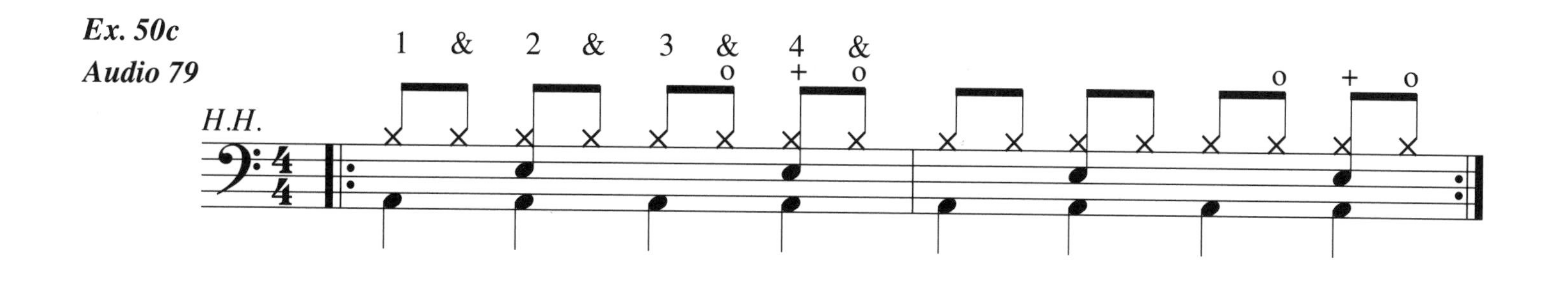

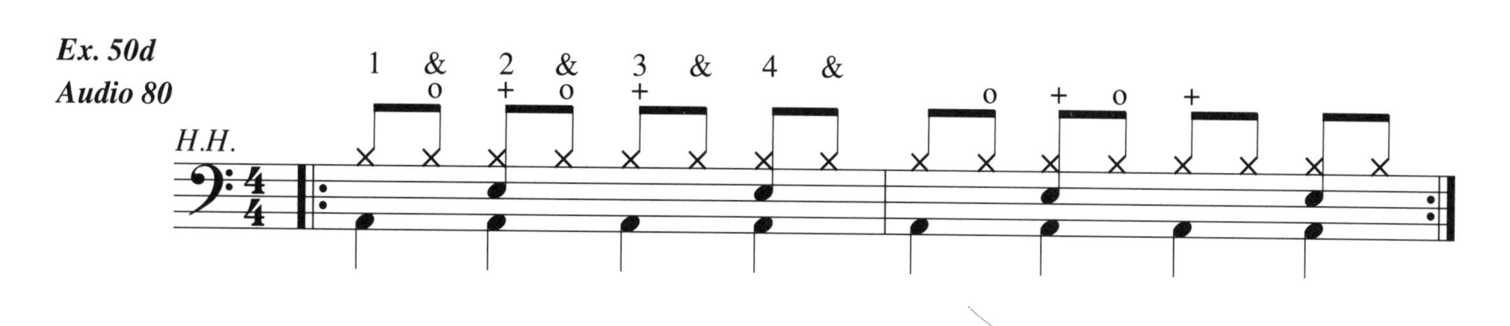

For extra practice try playing different bass drum patterns to each of these exercises.
Practise these exercises at different tempos, from 70 bpm to 120 bpm.

TIED NOTES

Exercise 51 Audio Track nos 81–83

A tie between two notes indicates only the first note is struck and allowed to last until the second note. So in bar one of exercise 51a, although you count 1,2,3,4, only beats 1,3, and 4 are struck.

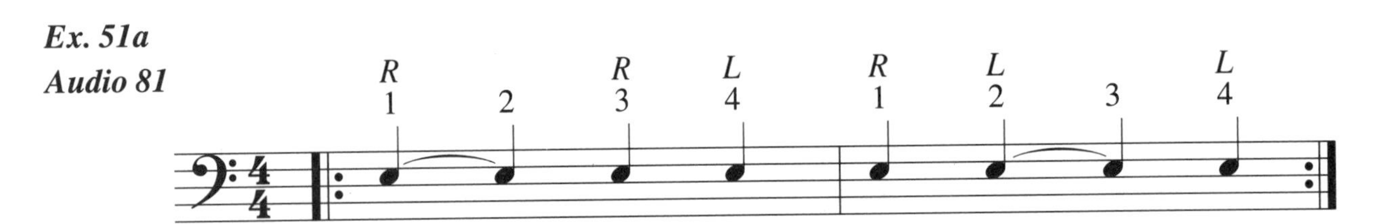

In exercise 51b we have two bars of eighth notes (which are repeated) with ties. Remember you only strike the first note of every two tied notes but continue to say the count.

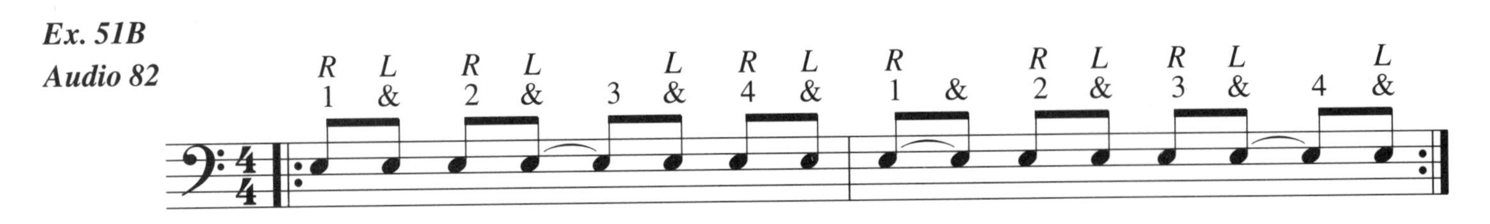

In exercise 51c we have a bar of sixteenth notes (which are repeated) with tied notes.

For extra practice play these exercises starting with your left hand (LRLR etc.).
Practise these exercises at different tempos, from 60 bpm to 120 bpm.

TIED NOTES (CONTINUED)

Exercise 52 Audio Track no. 84

In exercise 52 we have an example of tied notes being used within a rhythm. Note both the crash cymbal and bass drum are tied on the & of beat four.

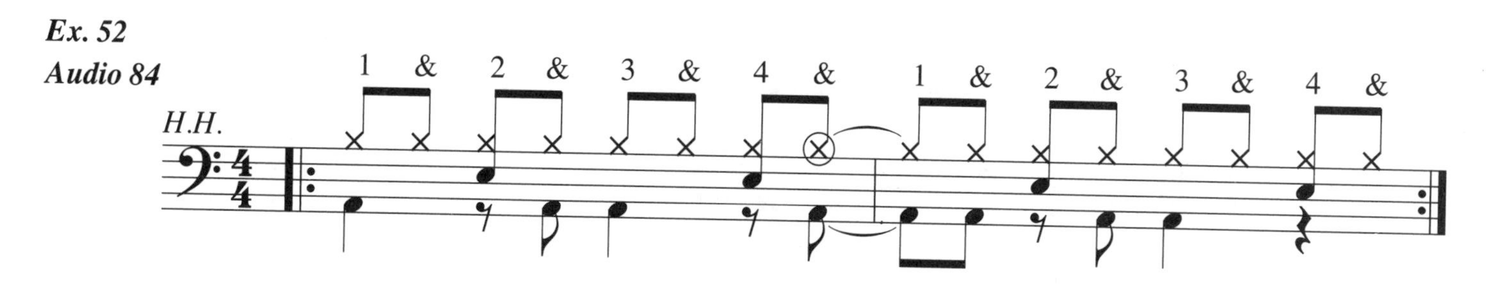

Exercise 53 Audio Track no. 85

In exercise 53 we have another rhythm using tied notes.

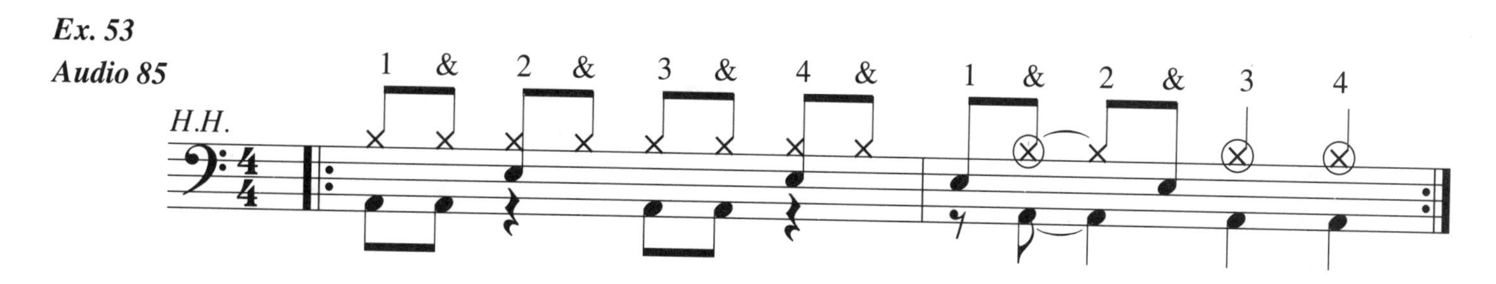

For extra practice alternate the cymbal pattern between the ride and closed hi-hat. Practise these exercises at different tempos, from 80 bpm to 130 bpm.

TIED NOTES (CONTINUED)

Exercise 54 Audio Track no. 86

In exercise 54 we have another example of using tied notes.

Exercise 55 Audio Track no. 87

In exercise 55 we have a two-bar rhythm using two tied notes.

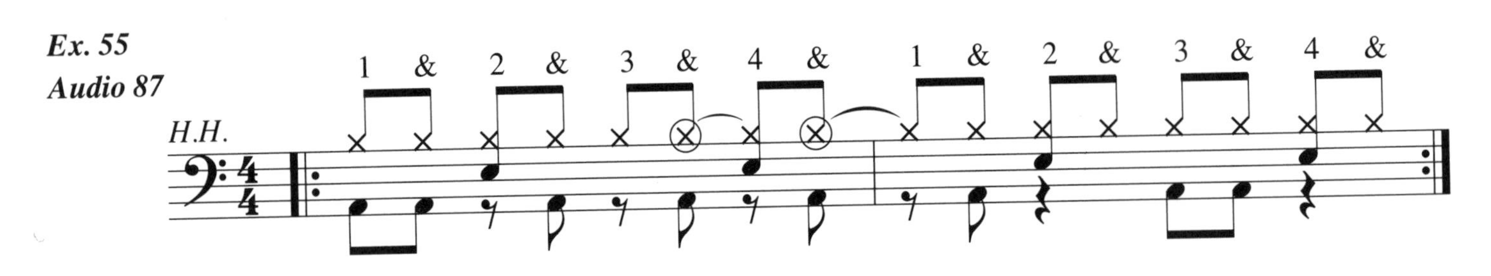

For extra practice alternate the cymbal rhythm between the closed hi-hat and the ride. Play eight bars of each pattern.
Practise these rhythms at different tempos, from 80 bpm to 130 bpm.

USING TIED NOTES AND OPEN HI-HAT RHYTHMS

Exercise 56 Audio Track nos 88 and 89

Exercise 56 is written in $\frac{4}{4}$ and consists of two parts (A,B).

In PART A we have a basic rhythm using open hi-hat beats as practised in exercise nos 48–50. Note the repeat signs at the beginning and end of part A.

Note the tied cymbal notes in bars seven and eight.

In PART B we play a similar rhythm but with an open hi-hat beat in every bar for the last eight bars. Note the accents over the last three eighth notes.

Ex. 56
Audio 88 + 89

Chapter 7

RHYTHMS IN DIFFERENT TIME SIGNATURES

Exercise 57 Audio Track no. 90

Exercise 57 is written in $\frac{6}{8}$. This type of rhythm is often used for slow tempo rock songs. Note there is a six-beat count into the first bar.

Ex. 57
Audio 90

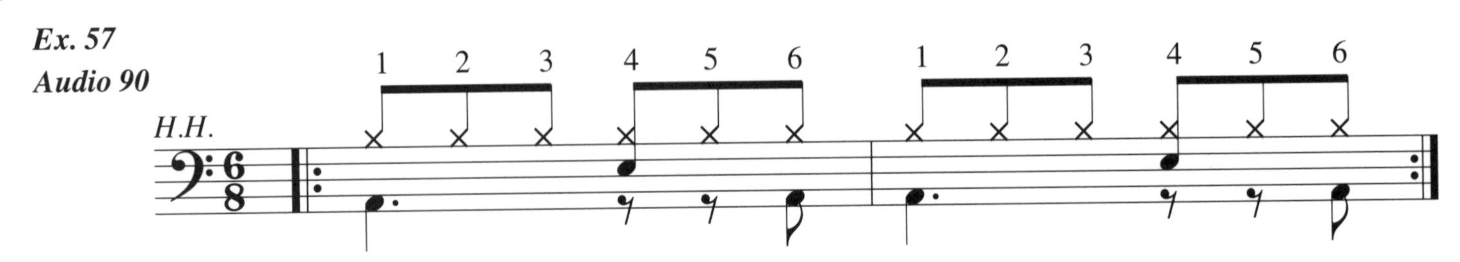

Exercise 58 Audio Track no. 91

In exercise 58 we have a two-bar rhythm in $\frac{6}{4}$. Note the closed hi-hat plays a quarter note pattern throughout. This rhythm would usually be played at a faster tempo than exercise 57.

Ex. 58
Audio 91

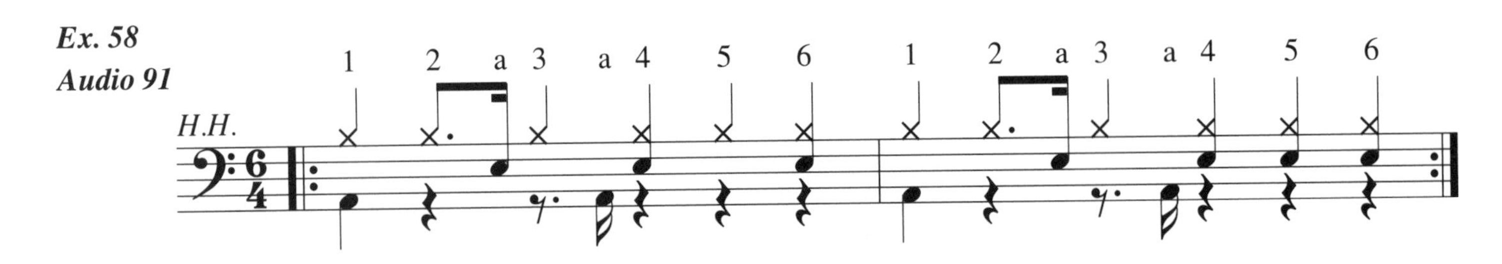

Practise exercise 57 at different tempos, from 50 bpm to 80 bpm. Note at these tempos each beat of the metronome will be equal to one eighth note cymbal beat.

Practise exercise 58 at different tempos, from 60 bpm to 90 bpm. Note each beat of the metronome will be equal to one quarter note cymbal beat.

RHYTHMS IN DIFFERENT TIME SIGNATURES
(CONTINUED)

Exercise 59 Audio Track no. 92

Exercise 59 is written in $\frac{12}{8}$. This type of rhythm is often used for slow tempo rock songs.

Note there is a twelve-beat count into the first bar.

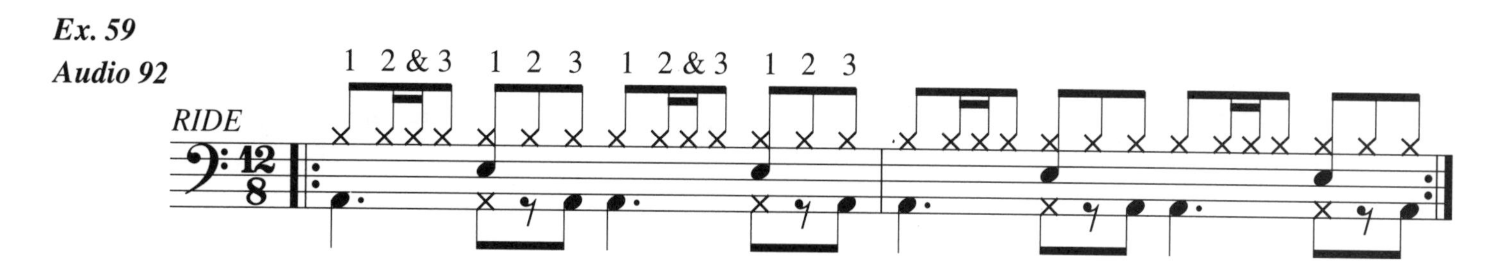

Exercise 60 Audio Track no. 93

In exercise 60 we have another rhythm in $\frac{12}{8}$. Note that in both these exercises the count is divided into four groups of three (4 x 3 = 12), as this makes it easier to count.

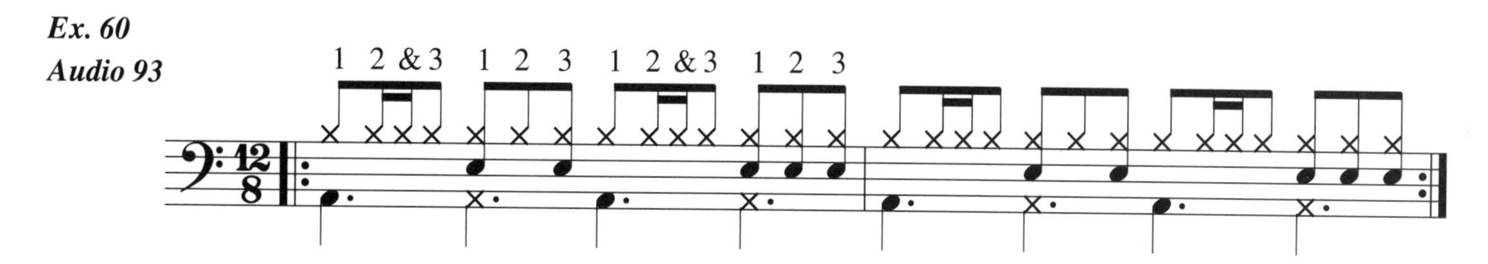

For extra practice play the ride cymbal pattern on the closed hi-hat.
Practise these exercises at different tempos, from 50 bpm to 90 bpm. Note that at these tempos each beat of the metronome will be equal to one eighth note cymbal beat.

RHYTHMS IN DIFFERENT TIME SIGNATURES
(CONTINUED)

Exercise 61 Audio Track no. 94

In exercise 61 we have a rhythm written in $\frac{5}{4}$. Note there is a five-beat count into the first bar.

Ex. 61
Audio 94

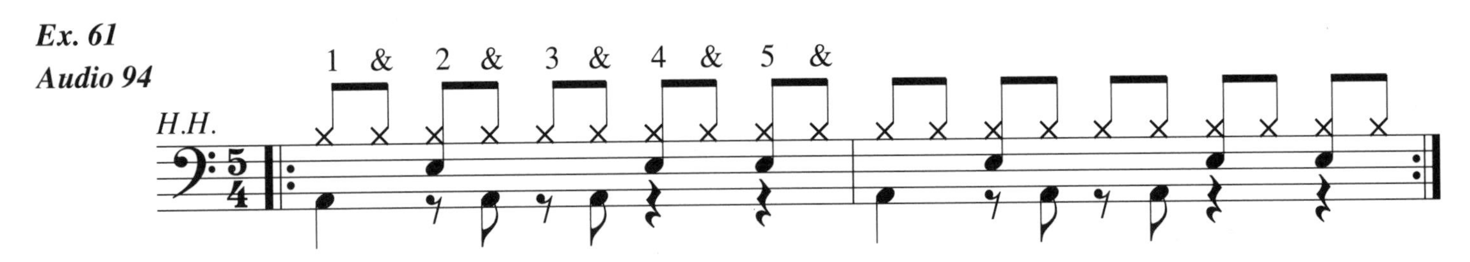

Exercise 62 Audio Track no. 95

Here we have another rhythm in $\frac{5}{4}$. The count for these rhythms could be divided into 1&2&3&1&2& etc. (3 + 2 = 5) as shown below.

Ex. 62
Audio 95

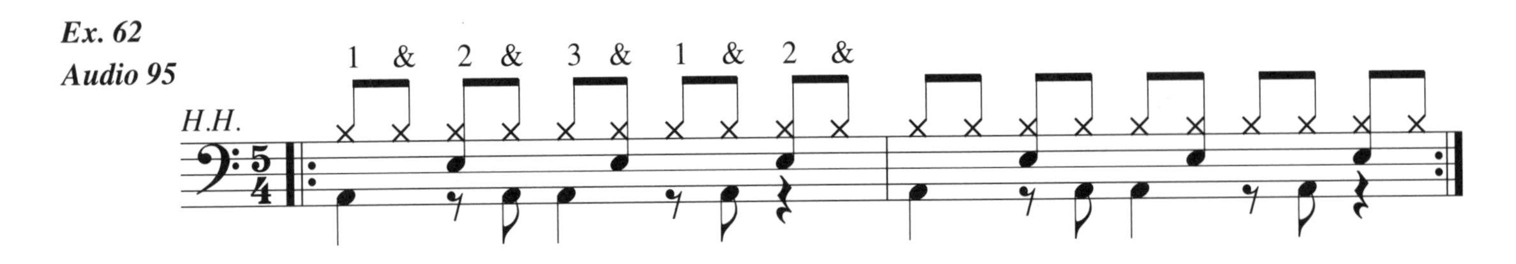

For extra practice play the closed hi-hat pattern on the ride cymbal.
Practise these exercises at different tempos, from 80 bpm to 120 bpm.

RHYTHMS IN DIFFERENT TIME SIGNATURES
(CONTINUED)

Exercise 63 Audio Track no. 96

In exercise 63 we have a rhythm written in $\frac{7}{4}$. Note that the count is divided into 4 and 3 (4 + 3=7).

Ex. 63
Audio 96

Exercise 64 Audio Track no. 97

Here we have another rhythm written in $\frac{7}{4}$. Note there is a seven-beat count into the first bar of both these exercises.

Ex. 64
Audio 97

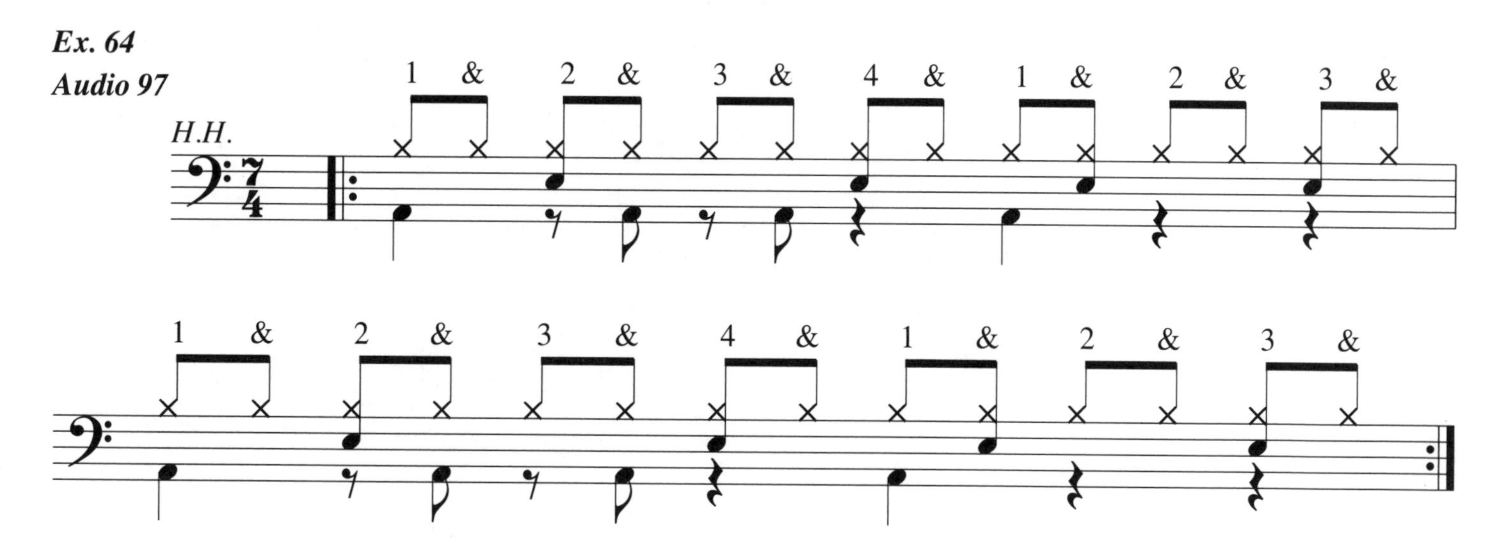

For extra practice alternate the cymbal rhythm between the closed hi-hat and the ride, play four or eight bars on each.
Practise these exercises at different tempos, from 80 bpm to 130 bpm.

USING RHYTHMS IN DIFFERENT TIME SIGNATURES

Exercise 65 Audio Track nos 98–99

Exercise 65 consists of three parts (A,B,C).

In PART A we have six three-bar sections (two bars of $\frac{4}{4}$ and one bar of $\frac{7}{4}$).

The count for the $\frac{7}{4}$ bars is divided into 4 and 3. Note the repeat signs.

In PART B we have eight two-bar sections (one bar of $\frac{4}{4}$ and one bar of $\frac{5}{4}$).

This part has a half time feel.

In PART C we move back to the hi-hat and play the rhythms as in PART A.
Note the tied cymbal notes in the last bar.

For a good example of songs played in different time signatures listen to SOUND GARDEN "My Wave", RED HOT CHILI PEPPERS "Breaking The Girl", TEMPLE OF THE DOG "Pushing Forward Back", and PINK FLOYD'S "Money".

Ex. 65
Audio 98 + 99
A
H.H.
1 & 2 & 3 & 4 &
1 & 2 & 3 & 4 & 1 & 2 & 3 &
B
RIDE
1 & 2 & 3 & 4 &
1 & 2 & 3 & 4 & 5 &

C
H.H.
1 & 2 & 3 & 4 & 1 & 2 & 3 &

SUMMARY

Having practised all the exercises in *How to Play Rock Drums* Parts 1 and 2, you will have gained a comprehensive understanding of reading and playing Rock Drums.

Throughout this book I have suggested tempos at which to practise (with the use of a metronome) each exercise. It is essential to be able to play every rhythm or fill at different tempos with confidence and without losing the groove.

For every musician (especially the drummer) keeping rock steady time within your playing is one of the most important roles to master.

Creating your own style of playing is also very important. This can be achieved over a period of time in many different ways. The tuning of your drums, selection of cymbals, choice of rhythms and fills, the way you strike the drum, all these things help to create your overall sound and style.

Take a listen to John Bonham with Led Zeppelin, Dave Abbruzzese with Pearl Jam, Mark Brzezicki with Big Country or Ginger Baker on his own albums. These are just a few drummers who have created their own recognisable styles.

So keep practising, enjoy your playing and one day your name could be added to the list!

To remove your CDs from the plastic sleeve, lift the small lip on the right to break the perforated flap. Replace the disc after use for convenient storage.